A Lone Black Gull

by

Michael Andrews

Books by Michael Andrews:

Poems for Amber
3 Begats
40 Turkeys So What
Xmas Tree Massacre
RiverRun
Not Another Love Poem
Machu Picchu
Riding South
A Telegram Unsigned
Gnomes and the Xmas Kid
The Poet from the City of the Angels
In Country (with David Widup)
The Gnomes of Uncertainty
Coffin Lumber

Some of these poems appeared in pervious books *Coffin Lumber, The Poet From The City Of The Angels, Gnomes & The Xmas Kid,* and *In Country,* and have first appeared or will soon appear in the following journals: *Aero-Sun Times, Aldebaran, Alley Cat Readings, Apostrophe, Arizona Quarterly, The Black Fly Review, Blue Unicorn, Broadside, The Chattaoochee Review, Contemporary Quarterly, The Dakalb Literary Arts Journal, Juice, Gallery Series, Le Beacon Review, The Long Story, The Margarine Maypole Orangoutang, Mr. Cogito, The Old Red Kimono, ONTHEBUS, Pacific Poetry And Fiction Review, The Roanoke Review, Saint Andrews Review, Samisdat, Screen Door Review, The Small Pond, The Smith, Snapdragon, Spillway, Spree, Tempest, Voices, Voices International, Wisconsin Review, Wormwood.*

First Edition

Library of Congress Catalog Card Number: 96-083336
ISBN 0-941017-49-4
Copyright © 2001 Michael Andrews
All photographs by the author.

BOMBSHELTER PRESS

Contents

PERIEGESIS GES

GNOMAE

COMING HOME

GNOMAE

THE PLACE WHERE I WILL DIE

GNOMAE

THE MULLAH AND THE PUSHER

GNOMAE

MACHU PICCHU

IN A SEA SHELL

MOST MEN

THE LAST WORD

To The Reader From
The Heart Of The Moment

The heart of stone beats slow.
The sky is ripe lemons bursting.
The storm licks its tongue through the mountain's
       fur.
The rain stalks across a summer lawn of hemlock
       and pine.
The sun mints gold on the hems of cloud.

Add S to a word and it cuts two ways.
It all comes down to a twig lying in the dust.
For a moment of your time
and an infinity of mine
the pulse of the mountain flutters
to the beat of the hummingbird's heart
and that twig is all there is of clocks and rulers,
the only moment that ever ticked,
the sum total of every thought,
all there ever was of galactic clusters,
the history of bipedal brains,
this poem —
            and you
reading this page,
closing this book,
putting it all back on the shelf

and walking out the door.

Foreword

Origin and Dedication

The first version of this book, titled *Gnomae*, was made by hand and I gave it to Flo on her birthday, November 27, 1996.

The numbered aphorisms on the title pages are taken from my book of philosophy, *"The Gnomes of Uncertainty."* The bulk of these poems span the years from 1965 to 2000 and are roughly grouped into chronological sections.

For Christmas 1995 Flo gave me a beautiful notebook. The gnomae that form the kernel of this collection were originally written in that notebook from 1996 to 1997. These later poems are contained in the sections titled *Gnomae* and in the last section, *Most Men*.

They were written as gifts for Flo.

On the Translation of Tu Fu

Late in life, around 769 c.e., Tu Fu wrote one of the great gems of human art, a poem variously titled *Travels By Night, Night Thoughts*, etc. It is the quintessential poem about the despair of a great artist who produced his work in good faith only to find his life over and all his artistic endeavors a failure. Additionally, Tu Fu did not himself have long to live. He was old, tired, sick and on a fixed and dwindling income.

The poem is essentially imagistic, that is the work of conveying the meaning of the poem is borne by the images rather than by statements of fact. The poem is also Chinese, which is to say that Tu Fu uses images that are predefined and commonly used in Chinese literature. This allows the poet to convey his meaning in a brief, telegraphic manner. This use of image depends upon a high-context culture. High-context presupposes that there is a great deal of information commonly assumed within the cultural context itself. For example a high context statement such as "Get the muffin bowl" assumes that someone already knows what the muffin bowl is and where it is located. A low-context statement assumes that such information must be conveyed as well; for example "Get the medium sized, green bowl on the left side of the third shelf in the cupboard to the left of and above the kitchen sink."

Contemporary American literature is low-context and traditional Chinese literature is high-context. Now, poetry itself tends to be high-context with much of its information implied within its cultural context and therefore inherently difficult to translate from one culture to another. On the other hand, a book of chemical formulae or a book of recipes tends to be low-context and most of the relevant information is stated explicitly.

In addition, the impact of this particular poem by Tu Fu depends on the reader knowing something about his life, as well as his contemporary cultural milieu and current events. These are components that cannot really be translated within the poem itself other than through the use of unobtrusive hints.

The one component of the poem that can be translated, or recreated, from the traditional Chinese to contemporary American English is the use of imagery. The Chinese tended to use abstract images that were predefined and commonly known to be metaphors or symbols that represented certain specific concepts. For example the phrase 'between Heaven and Earth' means, in the context of Tu Fu's poem, that he does not belong to life on earth among the living and he has no expectation of any reward after death, and it also can be taken to imply that his poetry and reputation will probably also disappear into oblivion.

Contemporary American literature tends to follow Wallace Stevens' advice on the use of concrete imagery. A specific example of a class is taken to represent the entire class. For example, Algernon the mouse may represent all mice, all rodents, all mammals, or an abstraction such as all life.

Concrete imagery makes the poem more accessible by asking its audience to actively experience a specific thing rather than being passively told about an abstract concept. It is the difference of actually having an experience as opposed to being told about an experience. The concrete image or event is a metaphor which triggers a real experience in the reader's mind, the idea, meaning, revelation or epiphany which the author intended to convey, but does not explicitly state. This is one of the most powerful tools available to the contemporary American poet. This power is bought at the risk of being imprecise, the risk that the audience will not make the connection from the concrete example to the correct abstract class. But then poetry is a risky business.

Although no one can translate the sum total of Chinese culture or even Tu Fu's life in a single poem, we can hope to translate the poem's imagery into the contemporary American idiom in order to make Tu Fu's poem accessible and alive to an English speaking reader. This is, for example, the reason that I chose to use the concrete images of 'between the mud and stars' instead of the traditional image 'between heaven and earth.' The traditional image has a more authentic Chinese feel, but the concrete image has a more powerful impact.

"Heaven" is a general metaphor that represents an abstract concept for immortality, the after life and the sky. "Stars," however, conveys more information: the action is at night and the sky is clear. Astrological objects are apparent. It is also a concrete image which implies the same abstract concepts of afterlife and immortality.

"Earth" is, again, a general symbol for the planet and its life, for terra firma and for soil, which is here taken to imply the origins of human life. "Mud," on the other hand, is specific. It also refers to the idea that human life springs from the soil and the river as a product of this world, not of heaven, and that we humans, like the moon, wish to leap to the stars, to immortality and to heaven.

Mud further reminds us that we are on a river. We are not in a building or in a city. Finally, mud is also a concrete image that represents our mortal human life.

I also chose to suggest some of the facts of Tu Fu's life within the poem. Some hint of the conditions that brought Tu Fu to such a state of despair needs to be more apparent to a non Chinese speaking audience who may not be familiar with his biographical history.

Tu Fu was, in a certain sense, far more fortunate than most poets. His work was preserved, later rediscovered and accorded its rightful place in the canon of the poetic arts. Most poets simply disappear into oblivion and, of course, Tu Fu was simply too dead to derive any personal satisfaction from such post mortem acclamation.

Still, his poem remains one of the great monuments to the human and artistic spirit. Tu Fu toiled at his art in good faith in spite of the world's indifference and in spite of every other sort of misfortune.

And that is the heroic endeavor in anybody's language.

A Comment on the Poems

There were several famous collections of gnomae complied in ancient Greece. They were moslty comprised of poets from the 6th century b.c.e.; Theognis, Solon, Phocylides, Simonides of Angoros, and others. But there were forms of gnomic poetry in the early Egyptian tradition, the Chinese Shih and Shu, and the Sanskrit Hitopadesa going back to the 2nd millennium. Later examples are the *Book of Proverbs*, passages from Greek tragedy and *Beowulf*. In time "gnomic" came to be applied to any poetry which deals with questions of ethics in a sententious fashion.

Most of the poems in this book are of three main types; gnomes proper, epiphanies and imagist poems. Their most common element is brevity. Although a few remain, I have removed most of the long poems even though some of those were, in effect, shaggy-dog epiphanies.

The long poems that do remain seem to me to be comprised of a series of ephiphanies or aphorisms, or the entire poem is itself an epiphany. Although every poem reflects a philosophical basis, or point of view, most poems refrain from making outright philosophical statements, which, in general, only weakens the poem. All the long poems that have been left in this collection do make philosophical statements.

The distinction between gnomes, epiphanies and imagist poems is based strictly on my own private definition.

A gnome is a short pithy statement, or aphorism, about some truth. Typical examples are "Know thyself," or "Buy low, sell high." In my mind the gnome proper is a general, abstract statement which is stated in a interesting way, often with a clever twist. An example from this book is:

MOST MEN

To live a moment
is to live forever,
except that few men
live at all,
and though no one
lives longer
than a dead child
most men
die infants.

An imagist poem is exactly that, it states its case in concrete images, which are metaphors for what the poet wants to say. The content or meaning is not stated in either an abstract or in a direct way, but is concealed in the image. The image, however, has a direct, experiential power that an abstract statement does not. In the pure imagistic poem the image is presented without comment.

AN OLD DRUNK

The earth presses
the old drunk
into the sky,
doubling him over
unconscious
on a bus bench.
His hat
topples
into the gutter.

The epiphany is a particular kind of poem defined primarily by its subject matter which is most often the metaphysical moment, the eternal now. Haiku is a typical example. These poems portray that eternal moment of peace, illumination and revelation. Epiphanies can use both images and abstractions, but most often lean toward the imagistic. Because they are often stating the ineffable, epiphanies can sometimes be surrealistic.

AN EVENT IN AUTUMN

A leaf falls,
the earth shakes.

I watch a spider
crawl into the fire.

The leaf flies
back into the tree.

Obviously, the majority of poems are mixtures of all of the above elements and do not fall absolutely into one type or another.

Most of the poems in this book are the kind of poem I would tell students not to write. Abstract statements easily become cliches and general, abstract statements are the most difficult to say in a new, or even a mildly interesting way.

The purely imagistic poem runs the risk of not conveying the meaning the poet intended, or worse, no meaning at all. Often the meaning is simply a vague feeling, mood or atmosphere, and if that is enough for the poet, then it remains for the reader to decide if that is enough for him.

The epiphany is always teetering on the edge of the trite. The metaphysical eternal moment is by definition and in principle, ineffable. So, to try to communicate what is not-communicatable is not only impossible, but it can only be done by suggestion and innuendo. Sometimes it works, sometimes not.

My apologies for those that do not. My thanks for those that do.

Travels By Night

a poem by Tu Fu, circa 769 c.e.
translated by the author

On shore a small breeze bends fragile grass.
I am alone. My mast tickles the belly of the
      night.
The stars fall down into the mud on the sad, vast
      plain.
The moon leaps to the stars from the great
      river's flow.
Words cannot save me. My name is lost with my
      poems.
I am old. I am sick. I have been retired from
      office.
My loved ones are lost on the river's current.
My words, my name and my self adrift, floating

between the mud and stars —

                  a lone black gull.

A
Lone
Black
Gull

Barnum Was Right

No one
ever went broke
underestimating
public taste.

No one,
I might add,
ever suffered
for underestimating
public intelligence.

No one ever reads me.
I haven't got a cent.

I can't figure out
what it is
that I am
doing right.

In The Beginning

1.0.1   A universe comes into being when a distinction is drawn.

1.0.2   A mind and its universe are one.

1.0.3   We do not know how we know. We do not know our purpose. We do not know where we are going. We do not know who we are. We are on an odyssey to meet our selves.

Most Men

To live a moment
is to live forever,
except that few men
live at all,
and though no one
lives longer
than a dead child
most men
die infants.

Sand Castles

We are an explosion of shovels
pails and heaving sand —
my brother and I build turrets,
massive walls, and moats
to divert the sea's attention.

It takes all day.

The next day
the sand is flat
as dead champagne.

A philosopher is born.

Gumballs

It takes a long time
to get 4 pennies.
It takes most of a summer
and it takes
sacrifice and patience
and now and then, a scam.
"Red," I say,
"I've got to have a red one."
The first one out is green
and I give it to Grubby.
Grubby will eat
any color he can get.
Blue is not so bad,
so I put it in my pocket.
I know I'm in trouble
when I get the orange one,
but Grubby doesn't mind a bit.
My last penny
falls into the slot,
I twist the knob around
and it clatters
through the gears.
The gumballs rumble
and I hear one
rattle down the chute.

"White," I yell. "I hate white."

White is no color at all.
White has got no taste.

It follows the other two
into Grubby's puffing cheeks.
My kid brother
drops in his only penny,
twists the crank,
pulls out a red gumball
and pops it in his mouth
and that's the way life is.

Blue — is not so bad.

Jelly Bean Machine

Pink is mint
and white is too
and green is lime
and yellow, lemon
and red explodes
strawberries
in my mouth
but best of all
black is licorice —
and no one else
will eat them.

Ah Life!

Less
than
meets
the
eye.

Untaught

No one learns
from nothing
and life
is more than willing
to withhold no lesson
and although
most men
have never learned
to learn
without
a teacher
no one
taught
me.

Ataraxia

The crabby old lady
who guards the coffee pot,
the little princes of bureaucracy,
the neutered worker bees,
the drones,
the kamikaze pilots in traffic,
the absurd morass of human seas,
of cultures dying,
idiotic opinions singe the air
like stars of falling mud,
hurtling nowhere,
through nowhere,
from nowhere,
and I act out my self
with mindless disengagement.

The game stops
when you cease
to catch the ball.

The Way

A wise man does not teach the end.
He teaches the way.
And he is not too serious
about that.

Viet Nam

2   All knowledge, language and certainty are bounded by the limit of paradox.

2.0.1   The foundations of reality are in paradoxical space and are in principle unknowable.

2.1.24.6 Sentience is the paradoxical boundary that defines a self.

2.1.24.7 A self is bounded by paradox.

The Fat Man
1945

Before they dropped it on Nagasaki
they signed their names
as though it was an object of art.
They put their wives and children's names on it
as though it were a gift from a loving cousin.
On 8 August 1945 they dropped
it out of a B-29 Box Car named *Enola Gay*
and killed 125,000 humans.
They merely injured another 150,000.
A few year later Klaus Fuchs,
a physicist in need of a vacation
and a Swiss Bank account
sold atom bomb secrets to the Soviets.

In school the siren screamed
and we had to crawl under the desk
to avoid the flying glass.
Flying glass seemed like the least
of our worries if our eyes
melted down our cheeks.

For every Einstein, we learn
there are a thousand Oppenheimers.

We are the bomb babies.

We know how the world ends.
It has nothing to do with a whimper.

The Old Hand

The plane burrows into the steam
and hits dirt in the Filipino night.
It is dark and hot and sweat
drips from the light bulbs
in the airport bar.
I sweat with all the dignity
an idiot can muster
wearing a tweed suit in the tropics.
In an hour or two the plane
will haul my naive self to
the Republic of Vietnam.
I drink something cold and sweet
like real men are supposed to do.
The older guy sitting next to me
is dressed in a frayed and crumpled
Hawaiian shirt, baggy pants
and dusty exhaustion.
He just came from the Nam,
going home with his dead eyes,
empty wallet and dying adrenals.
His voice echoes out of a hollow
tunnel, leading to alien landscapes.
We talk civil nonsense until
I find the crack to slip in my
only question, "What's Nam like?"

I can't see what he sees when
he looks at me, first mad, then sad.
He lets out a lungfull of tired breath,

swallows his drink and says,
"It'll grow on you,"
and walks out into the night.

Kowloon To Hong Kong

I cross on the Star Ferry from Kowloon to Hong Kong
white water surging forward at my feet
and the sea, grateful for my return—
black and gray storm clouds billow,
and pillar high above the city.
The island is silent, and waits for rain.

I stink of jungle and death.
The heat and stench of Nam
has plugged my nose with concrete,
carved my eyes into caves
where dragons breed and die.

The city tosses in her bed, dreaming of me.
She steams with lust as long as I am young.
She is as busy as a whore on Saturday night
changing money, sea traffic, buying and selling,
lights and music, taxis and pimps—
she is in the business of dreams come true.

The ocean's dark, menstrual wine sloshes
among the rocks and wharfs, the islands and trees.
Sea-going vessels, lightning and rain,
the night blankets the seething lust of the city.
She nestles into bed, wiggles her fanny, and waits for me.
I am on a hill watching her lights stutter and blink.
I am writing this poem for the city and its sea,
one more night closer to my death.

Saigon Sea Lanes

I swim in the people,
all brown and tiny—they bubble
and flow, ebb and swell into waves,
streams, floods and rapids,
bodies sweating and gushing,
the singsong of alien Jabberwocky,
magnetic women sway, bamboo like,
the smell and heavy sweetness of the air,
the decaying life and dying men,
the violence of pleasures,
the panting dogs of war,
the taxis roar unmuffled down Cach Mang,
the cyclos blow mountain banks of smoke,
the pedicabs weave and pump
through the traffic lanes—
a world as alien
as a Saturday morning cartoon.
I am exiled into chaos,
just another derelict cluttering
the sea lanes of humanity.
I drift with the tides,

a bottle without a message.

Cheating

Fuck these cards.
I scramble up the cards
and throw the deck on the table.

A man who cheats at solitaire
will cheat at life.

A man who cheats at life
has got his shit together.

Minnie And Mickie

Minnie and Mickey
are what the grunts call them.
They don't have real names
and they are brother and sister.
Minnie is 13 and once had a doll.
Mickey is 9 and used to be a child.

The grunts all took Minnie into the bush
for some quick pussy
and Mickey ran errands,
cleaned weapons, shined boots
and smoked with the GI's.
One day Minnie stepped on a mine
and they put all her parts
in a small plastic bag.
No one could find her pussy
for one last punch in the bush
but a few days later
Mickey is hit by a rocket
while smoking with the guys
and both his arms are blown off.
The medic tries to treat him
but the cigarette is still burning
in the fingers of the severed arm
and when it burns down to fingers
and burns them into charcoal
Mickey screams that he can
feel the burn and the medic
shoots home the morphine
and now the grunts

have to shine their own boots
and go in the bush
with five finger Mary.

Central Market & The Worm Doctor

I am shopping for mosquito netting and meat.
I buy netting from a little old lady
and by counting fingers, writing numbers
and talking pigeon. She agrees to sew it
into a canopy to cover my bed,
to keep away the mosquitoes
and the dreams and the night.

The meat hangs in the central market
like painted red penitents
kneeling at the doors of some heaven
no one will ever be good enough to enter.
The meat is swarming with flies
which they brush away when serious
money gets involved.
I buy a slab of mystery meat,
cheese from Europe and apples from Dalat.

Outside there is a medicine man —
the Pied Piper of Vietnam.
He has a small army of children
with or without nervous, shrieking moms,
squatting over yesterday's news
and he makes them drink the medicine
until they shit away runny turds
and all their intestinal worms.

I catch a cab and bicker over the fare
under the Prill Toothpaste billboard
and I think about my meat and the flies

and about taking the good doctor's medicine
and I hand the meat over to the driver as a tip
and have him drop me off at the Rex
for a sawdust and axle grease hamburger.

Better safe than sorry.

Willy Peter

"It fuckin' goes right through ya,"
Vinny shrieks at Peacenik
while his hands shake and fumble
at the compress wrapper
and Dinky watches a cloud
sail past the green, leafy canopy
his eyes have just faded away
the picture of the star burst
the white phosphorous blooming
like a time lapsed movie
of a fireworks flower
unfolding to the sun.

A case of friendly fire
his mind rolls around slowly.
The air strike was too close,
but then so was Charley
and he can hear Vinny screaming
about it goes right through ya
and he guesses that it has
something to do with him
but the cloud is somehow
the most profound thing that
he has ever seen, way beyond
the merely beautiful,
the way it drifts,
a galleon charting the seas
of heaven and he can feel
Vinny pushing on his chest
and the sucking way he breathes

but in the end
the cloud just
takes him

away.

Time To Write A Different Poem
Chatsworth, 10 Feb 93

I flew out of the Nam in March of 1971
13,396,320 heartbeats ago.

I looked all the way back
and my heart, a muscle engine
steadily pumped out the days.

If I squeeze my fist tight
just twenty times
my heart begins to ache.

I sit in the van
while the rain
tattoos the metal roof
more than all my tears
that will ever fall
and many more times
than my heart will ever beat.

I wonder if the goddamn thing
ever gets tired.

I give it a little coffee.
Just a love tap, really.
I check my watch —
720 heartbeats
to write this poem.

Cao Dai Temple

1969, The Nam

Along the Long Binh Highway there is a temple.
It's as big and splashy as an uptown Baptist church
and we ride in just to see what the local color is.

She is at least ninety and she doesn't do English.
Why should she? She couldn't make a dime in a tea bar,
the army can't draft her and many gods are on her side.
She tours us around and show us the holy stuff.

There is a mural above the door.
It shows all their saints doing their saintly bits.
There is Moses and Jesus and Buddha and Mohamed and
        Confucius —
the stench of gods is pretty rank in here.
The Cao Dai used to be one of the best
fighting machines in the land of Nam.
That's because they were believers.
Diem put them out of the fighting business.

Now they believe in free market enterprise
and they run the biggest opium and gun
running markets along the Laotian border—
a Sunday market for the heavy hitters.

I'd say they have covered
their bases, their bets and their asses.

Better safe than sorry.

4Day Tire Store
Los Angeles, 12 Feb 92

*"He (the District Chief) told them specifically that if they
did not personally see an incident, then it did not occur."*
Gloria Emerson, *Winners & Losers*

The rain boils on the pavement
like a sizzling monsoon in a distant jungle
in a war far, far ago.
It wept when it killed our joy there.
It weeps now as we rot
in this stinking, wet desert
while the rich folk scream in their canyons
about mud on the carpets,
rain in the mansion
and rust on the Beamer.

A child sits in the hot, green rain
in that far, far war ago.
Her stomach is an overripe mellon.
Her eyes are as dead as a sun baked trout.
Her legs are broken pencils.
Her clothes would not survive a modest washing.
Her death doesn't make a sound
as it falls in the forest of broken lives.
No one hears her final sigh,
so no one asks if someone really died
until the rain boiled the pavement today

and I looked out the window.

Three Frosty Beers

His watch quit breathing at 7:13 p.m.
but Randolph John Webber keeps it up
for another 11 hours and 37 minutes.
If he knows that both his legs
have long since been tagged and bagged
to him it is just another morphine dream
in a carousel of a thousand dreams.

The clerk has put in a twenty hour day
and a clerical error in the scheduling
of flights results in a delay
of over four hours in Randy's
arrival at the triage in Pleiku.
His final dream is of a girl named
Cindy, a broken shoe lace on his
worn out sneakers and the urgent
need to wax his Mustang convertible.

The burned out clerk skips his dinner
in favor of three frosty beers,
consults his Seiko diving watch
and calls it an early night.
The Mustang convertible rusts into
a junk yard burial waiting for its wax.
Randy's brother Charlie inherits a pair of
sneakers with one broken shoe lace.
The sun throws a shadow from Washington's
monument the way a child points
a finger at something on a wall.
In the summer, around 6:50 a.m.,

the shadow points to Randolph Webber's
name etched into a granite wall.
Cindy marries three times
and can't remember love.
Her first born son grows a scraggly beard
and cannot recall his father's smile.

Gnomae

Living In La

I live in a hot dry, desert
with iodine sunsets
lead skies
and fogs of acetone and ash.
We suck the rivers dry
running from the Sierras
and water what green we have
and I think of Tu Fu
sailing in the night.

I am one of the dead faces
behind the sooty windshields
on the 405 freeway
and behind the red lights
waiting for the green light
with the burned out bulb.

I had a heart once—
blood and muscle
and obsessive pumping.
One by one the universe
painted me pictures of
reasonable dreams and
the ludicrous promises of life.
The price is always
a chunk of heart and
one by one the universe
takes things away.

I was a poet once

and the conferences
and the academics
and the publishers,
the coteries, the high priests
cut it out of my heart
and replaced it with a scar
which rhymed with literary
allusions and critically correct.

I made money once.
I have nothing left
but Master Card threats in the mail,
income below the poverty belt,
no IRAs in the bank,
too old to hire,
no paid holidays to the Caribbean,
nothing but the poverty
of a thousand scars.

I was a philosopher once
and the same mob
strangled me
with a rope
twisted from
rags and idiocy.

My heart beats
a funny tune now,
more like a Model A
with dirty plugs.

I was an athlete once,
strong, straight and easy with grace

but an officer and a gentleman
turned my leg
into an unsalted pretzel.
Now I walk like a three legged camel.
Dysentery and stress,
yeast and bad food
stole the engine of my life,
turned my body
into a car battery
with two dead cells.

I was an artist once
and I was fool enough to believe
that artists made art.
Artists go to parties.
I am no good in a crowd
and the crowd
left my pictures on the wall
and bought the wallpaper instead.

I used to believe in love
but love brings terror
and nights of frozen black snot.
It brings pain and deprivation,
and sorrow
and more love.
Love brings its sister,
the princess of isolation
and bleeds the color
from the day
like a TV with a dying tube.
Love is the prison
we choose to die in

and love is all I've got.
It is our goodness
that mortars
the prison stones
around us.
It is our decency
that buries us
under mud and plastic flowers.

I had dreams once
but one cold, wet morning
the universe
walked outside
into it's garden
with a cup of hot coffee
steaming in its hand
and smashed each joy
and every dream
beneath its boots
like the soft crunch
of so many snails
crawling from the dawn.

The universe just keeps
taking things away
one by one
until I am as naked
as a rich man's baby
waiting my turn
in the oven at
the White & Day mortuary.

The young men prowl the streets

with their vibrant dreams
and their straight legs.
They live high and drive Porsches
or they live poor and
clutch their poetry books
but it all comes down the same—
you burn a page of poetry
or you burn a dollar bill
and it's the same pile of ash.

The last of my joy drove off
the way a Mustang five point oh
leaves my Nissan wagon in the dust.

Now I drive the freeways
of this dying town
in my gutless Nissan,
just so much ambulatory ash
looking for a brass urn.
When I'm gone
turn me into ink
and print the poems
you pissed on
while I still
could catch my breath.

I hope it's not too much longer.
The world is as vast and empty
as the eyes of a presidential candidate
and I am just another dead weight
tromping down some other clay
that is still trying to climb
up to touch the stars.

I am just a worker cog these days.
I typeset the words
of poets with brighter futures,
print their books,
pay the bills
and watch sitcoms at night
until the saccharine
aftertaste of oblivion
takes me down.

Poetry never saved a soul.

Before they pull my plug
and burn my words
there are only two rules
worth the waste of ink—
Give no pain.
Take no shit.

Everything else is a soundbight.

You can't break my heart.
It is only scar and snot
and the black dreams
of frozen cinder.

I have loved life
too much.

Baseball Caps

I use words of one syllable only
when speaking to men in baseball caps.
If the cap is rotated backward
I just grunt, use hand signals
or speak in cliches,
the current euphemisms,
hip platitudes
and sports analogies.
If they are lip reading the sport section
or are mentally disengaged
in front of televised sports
I avoid contact entirely.
Usually the mouth is agape,
saliva trickles south on a recessed chin
and the veins are roping
along the neck and temples.
Women in baseball caps terrify me.
Backward or forward,
they look both cute and smart.
They look like they are about to
give me five dollars
to wash the windshield
of their BMW convertible
or hold their place
in the ATM line.
Whether or not
I need the five dollars
I shut my mouth
and do what I am told.

On The Heads Of Pins

They still do it.

Funny little men with funny little minds
speculate on such nonsense
as Angels dancing on the heads of pins.

A thousand years ago
it was a serious question,
counting dancing Angels
the way we total traffic fatalities.

It takes that kind of mind.

They knew that there was only
so much dancing space
on all the heads
on all the pins
that were ever likely to be.

And because we all want
to dance on the heads of pins

they created hell.

The Pearl

I am the pearl of my pain.
I wear a beat up Chevy van
and old flannel.
I cannot find my smile.
Slick pricks dressed
in Jaguars and Armani
never frown.
I never understood
a thing.

The Fortune Cookie

The old man in Fook Gin's
is eating Tomato Beef,
putting away the steamed rice,
sipping oolong
and a hint of jasmine..

The moths beat around the paper lantern
painted with Chinese ladies and parasols.
The roaches crawl from table to table
looking for the Number 3 Special.

He finishes the Tomato Beef.
The fortune cookie comes with the bill.
He cracks it open, reads his fortune
and looks around at everyone in the place.
He looks tired and after a while he falls asleep
with his fortune in his hand
and his head beside the remains of the Tomato Beef.

Everything else keeps on doing what it always does
the roaches crawl, the moths flutter and beat,
and the Chinese ladies with parasols
stare out of paper lanterns.

I leave a tip, pay the bill and go home.

For the old man, that cookie
was his last fortune.

Fly In Amber

I first began to turn sad
about ten years ago.
Now I am sad whenever
I let my mind
see its own reflection
or bump into a self-portrait.
I work hard in order
to prevent my mind
from being caught
alone with itself.
I am a fly
caught in the amber
oozing between
cunning and chance.
We feel impotent
because our dreams
are too simplistic,
caught in the webs
of a universe
paralyzed with
all the wishes
of every other
dreamer.

Periegesis Ges

7.5   It goes unnoticed that it is a conflict of interests
        to allow lawyers to create the law.

7.5.2   Law is created by the powerful to control the
        weak.
            Both law and ethical codes are means of
        force.
            Law is, in principle, anti-democratic.

7.6.5   The imminence of apocalypse may be judged by
        the ratio of lawyers per capita.

Trusting Dreams
5 July 71, Perth

Bitter black, the night drips tar
and cold fingers tickle my throat.
This is not a hot Vietnam night
but the war drips from my fingers.
We joggle along the Canning highway
trusting our lives to bus 101
looking at the lines of brick houses,
some lit, some dark, strung
along the road.
Each set of roof and walls
an embattled stronghold
of dreams of peace,
the desperate vaults of hope.

Flo's friend invited us.
She is red haired, young
and painfully shy.
The party is polite
and the people are kind.
We haven't got a thing
to say to one another.

We are more alike than not,
needing all this brick and light
to keep away the
fingers of the night.

Black and bitter
and quiet as a stalking snake,

soaking wet air and cold sheets—
if you are awake, late,
and the vacuum of night
wants to suck you into dreams,
let it. Trust your dreams,
good or bad, and think of the sun
rolling through its black vacuum,
rolling toward you.

Another day dissolves in cold sheets.
Sleep takes me by the throat.

A Desert Of Talc

7 July 71, Australia

I am a desert of talc.
The pools of sorrow,
the dried up tears
and the swamps of pity
have been replaced
by parking lots
and shopping centers.
The petty agonies of life
are for sale,
two for one
in a dime store window.
It has been a long time
since I have wept
for anything but true
and sudden beauty.

Human culture
is a land-fill
of broken dreams.

Without warning
I like a stranger's smile.

Indian Ocean

13 July 71

Old men bury secrets in coffee cans.
I watched the young men die
like so many fleas in a fog of bug spray.
The Republic of Vietnam
and sheer human evil exterminated them.
So I sit on this deck chair
bobbing on the Indian Ocean and
I watch the old men stagger along
with their burdens of secrets
and histories that will
scatter in their ashes.
I wonder if their unsteady bodies,
were ever like mine,
strong and easy with grace.
How they endure the winter
is a mystery to me.

I build bridges
to span those years,
to prepare against that time
when I too will be caged
in a dying body and
an indifferent world.

The Nam buried the young.
It swallowed the weak, the old,
the sick, the dying and the passerby.

Sooner or later

a man is
his own
burial ground.

Collecting Charts

I collect charts and study maps,
plot courses,
always moving,
never leaving,
jealous of every place
that I have never been.

The Champagne Tea House

16 July 71, Kuala Lumpur

The afternoon monsoon turns the sky to coal.
It falls sudden and heavy and the world
turns small and quiet and a little less busy.
The umbrellas unfold like daisies in the sun
and we splash through the streets in sweaty rain jackets.
My leather moccasins turn green and rot away.

The streets are alive with charcoal fires,
all those people that have something to do
and places to go and the vendors hawking,
the hungry eating, and the rest shopping.

We hide from the rain in The Champagne Tea House.
Syrup tea, sweet and thick,
comes in heavy cups and saucers, white
and red and they say The Champagne Tea House.
The monsoon rain falls, soft and continuous,
the afternoon lingers, sweet and thick.

A small Malaysian girl
washes dishes on the sidewalk.
She is enchanted with my beard.
A small boy stands at my shoulder
and watches this sentence progress on the page.
I watch the people watching me,
eat the bitter-sweet food
and listen to the foreign chatter.

Great claps of thunder
punctuate the time.
The Indians eat with fingers,
the Chinese with chop sticks —
I eat with eyes and ears,
and time is in no great hurry —

time does not flow at all.

The Thai Song Greet
22 July 71, Bangkok

The busses have no apparent destination.
The traffic is all chaos, frenzy
and unsportsmanlike conduct.
This in the ugliest city I have ever seen.
It is a Sears and Roebuck reproduction
of oriental mist, bamboo and sampans —
a sprawling Asian imitation Los Angeles.

We locate the fabled Thai Song Greet hotel,
an establishment known only to the elite.
Filthy wooden tables and dirt cheap food
covered with a perpetual and inscrutable slime.
Happy Thais shuffle through the dust
making little clouds and dustdevils.
They are happy because foreigners will pay
big bucks for food the Thais wouldn't
feed to their dogs.
A horde of mangled, starving cats compete
for my plate of slime and eggs.

We sip tea for one baht a glass.
It is strong and sweet,
the crystal sugar stirring patterns
in the milk brown goo.
We are compiling lists of cheap hotels;
compiling stories, dark adventures,
comparing notes with travelers from
Japan, India, Africa, Europe,
recalling the places that were beautiful,

the places that were serene.
We are all trading information
so we can find that next plate of cheap slime.

We are here to buy fake press cards
and student IDs from the hungry rats
that lurk in the deeper shadows, the darker corners —
world weary French colonials,
vaguely sinister, exuding fake auras
of danger and charismatic untrustworthiness.
In truth they are petty men with petty dreams,
victims of petty addictions and petty crimes.
They are willing to buy, sell, or trade
any service at a cost.
We stretch our aching backsides,
idly sip the tea, waiting for the rain
to let the day trudge on to its death.
Between us, we have seen nearly all
the world there is to see.
We couldn't come up with a single truth between us.
Wandering is not growth, but expansion —
the patterns of crystal horizons
lead us on with fake promises,
false IDs and idle curiosity.

Somewhere, we fantasize,
someone has it good.

I sip my tea, the crystal sugar stirs
false patterns in my mind —
the rain is unwilling
to surrender the afternoon.

Reclining Buddha

23 July 71, Bangkok

The Buddha reclines in Wat Po.
He is gaudy and gold
and smiling in repose,
a divine Kewpie doll.
He is musing on the simple minded
gullibility of the tourists.

We meet a monk named Harn.
He is young and friendly.
He wants us to visit his monastery.
I've been a monk and I've seen monasteries
and we haven't got the time.

The Buddha smiles timelessly
and his gold leaf peels,
revealing mortal brick.

Graves By The Ganges

Belur Math, Calcutta

The prayer passes from temple to temple,
a baton in a relay race to paradise.
The relics of those who are revered
are preserved and wait for adoration.
They gather in the gloom of years.
They are avaricious for the dust.

Receptacles of ash, tombs of men,
dressed in flowers, gardens among
the grass and graveled walks.

August bones, deep in earth,
contemplate the flight of
a solitary bird.

Kamarpukur

The Siva temple next to Pyne's house
is crumbling in decay, but
it is beautiful even in its death —
the vine climbs the wall
and a vivid green moss clings
to the crumbling brick.

One by one, the gods
reclaim their temples.

A Small God

Kamarpukur, India

I go into the local shop
dirt floor, thatch roof
filled with strange gods,
misshapen and rustic brass
tortured and twisted
with three thousand
years of worship.

I buy a small god
riding on an elephant,
bearing the universe
on his shoulders.

He fits into my pocket.

Words Scatter

3 Aug 71, Kamarpukur

After puja
the devotees scatter in the night,
leaves blown from the trees.

I eat wheat porridge with Vitasokananda,
our words scatter in the night,
our silence waiting for the dawn.

Gadai's Mango

3 Aug 71, Kamarpukur

I wanted a leaf from the mango planted by Gadai.
It is forbidden to pick them otherwise the tree would
just be naked limbs bleached against the sky.

In the charcoal and furry dusk I walk by
without a thought in my head —

a leaf falls into my path.

Without Words

Puja is over.
Swami reads in Bengali.
I don't understand a word
and so, for me,
it is a music spoken without words,
a chant in the silent, village night.

He has been with us all day
showing us the sacred places,
the cultivation of his fields,
his fruits and vegetables,
and the mackerel caught in the tank.

He takes us to his garden
and gives us each a rose —

music without words.

The New Delhi Blues Again

The afternoon light melts
into evening shadows.
The lady who picks lice is going home.

Exotic geographies map my mind.

The cow follows her tether home
and night sets the pace in the streets
and the unlooked for cool.

Every exile seeks blots of color on a map
isomorphic to the bits and chunks of self.

Reflections in the street puddles
and random memories take me home.

A man's geography is his own place of exile.

I Am Painted In The Window
17 Aug 71, New Delhi

I am as sick as a Calcutta trash dog.

I sit by the hotel window
and time and life
and India and age
flow by on the streets below.

I spend my time
staring out of the hotel window.
The people in the street below
think that I am a painting on the glass.
On my side of the window I'm real.
On either side of the glass it is
here and now, and India revolves about me
unmoving in this great chaos of movement.

The picture of the sick me
on the inside of the glass smiles back.
This is no time for reflection.
The slow creep of the disease
brings reality into sharp focus —
the frailty of the body,
the reality of the flesh.

My body is still young, still graceful.
But in the street, age rolls on,
time pushes like an angry commuter,
taxis with forward gears only,
old men falling from step to step.

I have no patience with sickness,
this horrible, blood-sucking,
breath-wheezing and head-swirling weakness.

A taxi misfires its way down the street,
clatters through its gears,
flows into traffic,
turns the corner,
and disappears.

Happy Feet

It is monsoon season.
The rain comes every day
and my shoes turn green,
then fall off.

I judge hotels by the toilet.
If it doesn't flush
I know I am paying the right price.

The most useful possession in India
is a good pair of shoes.
Sandals work best.
Socks do not stay dry or clean.
You just need something between
your soles and the cow shit.

A happy man is a man with happy feet.

Austrian Tea

7 September 71, Graz

We back track Alexander's march
across Central Asia
and ride the bus into Graz, —
civilization at last —
and it takes enough money to buy
a day's worth of food
to buy a single cup of tea
with a twist of lemon in it.

For three years I've lived
on a dollar a day for food.
Fifty cents is outright theft
for hot water and dried leaves.

In Asia you only get cheated
if you are an idiot.
In a Western democracy
the rich cheat everyone equally.

Getting Lost

Wiedenbruk

The road goes on from
X on the map.
Feet slap the pavement,
holding down the earth
and no one knows where
the last step falls.

The great adventure
is getting lost.

Moments, Linz

The silhouette of a tree, limb naked,
against the autumn sky at dusk.

The solitary figure walking in a field,
a human molecule on a path of destiny.

The slow spread of fog
in the misted light of dusk,
drifting, creeping,
covers up fields and trees,
a sheet spread out for night.

The old man
walking down the road,
the shamble of old age,
the cessation of the day,
going home to sleep
the sleep of patience
and exhaustion.

A time of utter peace —
a moment gripped in
the terrible jaws of beauty,
the kind of moment
we hope
to die in.

White Death

3 Oct 71, Garmisch

The first snow
falls into trees.
The white agony of winter
drifts down,
shrouds the colors
of autumnal death.

Beside the road
an ice-clear stream
races over frozen stone —
white foam,
pale green,
colder than snow,
more talkative —

the water's song —
quiet snow —

I have never really lived at all.

Linz Again

4 Oct 71

The earth is round —
where can the wind be going
in such a hurry,
shaking the trees, rattling leaves,
gusting through the window,
acting like an angry bull?
It does not seem to care
that it is night,
that it is late,
that it is time to rest.

It is bringing me tales,
ancient stories, far off events.
It brings the desire
to be free and elemental,
to dance with a falling leaf.

I am so much clay that
managed to stand above the dirt,
a victim of my dreams.

The Woman Walking, Vienna
7 Oct 71

Her footsteps slap the naked path,
empty as a dead man's shoes,
kick aside the autumn leaves,
beside the muffled clatter of the brook.
She passes with the wind.

The leaves launch themselves
from the limbs of the trees.
The path, yellow and anxious, moves on.
The brook, eager for news, flows by.
The wind, crazy for stars, blows away.
The woman, pursuing dreams, walks by,
her footsteps die and fade into
that other world hidden on the far
side of a wall of fog.

I have never been there.

I am here,
buried in yellow,
littered with leaves,
counting steps —
going nowhere.

More Morning Fog, Salzburg
12 Oct 71

Fog, the hot breath of earth
on a cold, frosted morning.
We are hidden in the forest.
It is most quiet when the fog
builds walls and we do not speak.

Klenovika

28 Oct 71, Yugoslavia

All the way from the mountain
to the sea I was hoping to finally
understand a single simple thing.
Any simple thing.
Something like — why are bad men happy?
Why do dogs like humans?
Where do lost socks end up?

Now I'm just tired and I don't
understand a thing.
I am waiting in this desolation
beside the sea. I am waiting
and the wind is trying to blow me away.
It is a terrible strength,
blowing white caps, spray and milky mist
back out to sea faster than the waves
can roll into shore.
It is ripping at trees and brush,
tearing at our tiny bubble of stillness.

I am waiting because I don't understand
why I am here, why I am waiting,
what I am waiting for.

Nothing comes —
only the wind
and I have never seen
the wind so angry.

Any Passing Wind, Dubrovnik
30 Oct 71

Men dream like trees
tapping roots.

Men desire permanence,
clutching earth.

We were never the root.

We are only the leaves
at the mercy of
any passing wind.

Strimonilos Kolpos

6 Nov 71, Greece

A bird flies into the windshield of the bus,
catches its wing in the wiper,
and speed and the wind
tear out its life.

It was no bigger than a plum,
with yellow markings,
and with great convulsions
it beat out its small life
in the palm of my hand.

It just pisses me off.

When we get to the beaches
above Thessaloniki
I strip down for
a swim in the surf.

When I run down to the sea
the dolphins come
and swim in circles
leaping and diving
stitching the surf
to the sky.

The dolphins and I
hold a wake for the tiny bird.

And then it is time
to be glad
to be alive.

Delphi

11 Nov 71

We drive past the Isthmus,
past Corinth, and late in the day
come to Delphi, looking
down the cliffs to the sea.

The tourists forgot to come
so we have the ruin to ourselves.
It is as silent as the oracle —
only the goat bells
play soft music,
carried away in the
sough of the wind,
the dance of the trees.

We sit on the highest row
in the theater and listen
for words from the god.

Words do not contain
the ecstasy and words
can not endure the light.
They whither under the strain
like dahlias under snow.

It is a sad thing
that they are so fragile,
that they do not bridge
that slender gap
that divides you from me.

In the end, words
also failed the god.

We climb down the mountain
and into the bus.

The goats settle down
for the night.

Herse, Goddess Of The Dew

In the morning
I gather the goddess
from the flowers
and like a fool
I drink
her nectar
hoping
to stop
the sun.

Kastelli, Crete
1 Dec 71

The island is silent, watchful
as a cat about to spring,
waiting beneath the threat of the storm,
waiting for the thunder,
the slash and arc of the lightning,
and even the water is still,
silent as worship
before the unveiling of a mystery,
but the wind leaves the footprints of some
god stalking across the waves.

There is a power in the island.
It is ancient and female.
I can feel the power growing with the moon
and it is dark and hidden
as all things of the earth are,
deep, unknown and concealed.

My tiny filament of fate
twists in the dark mother's fingers,
but I am a man
and I have always worshipped the sun.

The Cretan Goatherder

We wake up in the morning by the river
that ties the mountain to the sea at Agia Nikolaos.
The old goatherder comes down every morning
to our camp on the beach.
He waters his sheep and goats
at the stream, and watches the morning sea.

He is Cretan—
the mustache like the wings of a hawk,
boots marching up the thigh—
taller than I am and strong.
"Calimera," I say
and he says the same
and something more
that I can't understand.
My Greek isn't much
and I say some English
that he doesn't understand
and it doesn't much matter.

I give him a stool.
He crosses his legs and lights his pipe,
and I offer him some tea with honey—
for him, the honey is special.

We sit there and sip tea
sometimes an hour without talk.
Then he says "Effreesto"
and he and the goats,
dogs, rams and sheep

go up the mountain.

Today I show him a world map.
He's never seen one before
and he keeps pointing
to America and Russia
and then at Kriti,
laughing at the size of it.

We never ask each other's name.
But we say things
on these silent mornings
that can't be put into Greek
or English or poems.
Things that have to do
with being alive
with sharing tea and honey
with looking out to sea
on autumn dawns
saying nothing.

Vision On A Sunlit Road, Crete

We are driving along the north side of Crete
with a bus load of hippies and drug freaks
who are picking olives for room and board.

I drive from turn to turn,
in and out of deep shadows and pools of sunlight
and time passes from curve to curve
and it comes to me here,
the little ecstasy,
that moment without an I,
when there is no difference
between me and the roadside oak.

If I say a word the moment will die.
Everything falls short of vision.
The moment dies anyway
and the tree is just a tree
and I am left
only who
I am.

Cemetery Of Keramikos

Dust, mud and stone,
a museum plundered from the grave,
mementos of the dead,
a forest of stone —
headstones are the flowers
of ash and bone.

There is a stone relief
of a woman looking at her jewels
for the last time.

In the moment before death
her last thought was for her jewels.

I feel sorry for the fool
who bought her with
a handful of baubles
and a lifetime
of cheap trinkets.

Flesh And Stone

14 Nov 71, Athens

In the Agora at Athens
there is a marble head
of a goddess.
Alone, I caress her face
with my hands,
making love, flesh and stone,
I even kiss her cold, stone lips
thinking that this would
bring her to my dreams.
In that brief orgasm
of blood and marble
she fails to bring me
back to life.

Calais

21 Dec 71

Nothing drives a man to philosophy
faster than an angry woman.

Bottom Line

2 Feb 72, New York

I can't say why any two people
end up stitched together,
the patched rags of a quilt,
among these ruins and devastated lives,
out of all these cities and rootless people
and all the hungry subway cars.
I don't know if the net result
of what we bring to one another
is pleasure or pain.

We have agreed on love,
and it's good enough for me.

Gnomae

7.6.13.4.3 The irony is that anti-abortion fanatics who espouse the rights of the unborn are more than willing to not only ignore the rights of the children of other nations, but are perfectly happy to remove the economic rights of the future generations of the unborn.

7.6.13.6.1 Secrecy, or the possession of and access to information, has always been the tool of a predatory elite.

7.6.14.42 Free market predation is the best example of a cultural system gone insane.

7.6.14.42.1 Cultural insanity is defined as a system created by humans that works only to fulfill its own needs and agendas, and no longer works to achieve human needs and purposes.

Drones

If you are interested in the kind of man
who has contributed nothing
to the evolution of the species,
nothing to the welfare of others
adding nothing to the fact that
he eats, shits, procreates and dies,
and still is spoiled rotten
with wealth and fame
then open any
sports page.

Syllogism

If youth is wasted on the young
then justice is wasted on the law
and power is wasted on the privileged
and most certainly, wealth
is wasted on the rich.

At The Movies

We sit in the pitch black of the Mann Six theater
full up with dull normals chewing Snicker bars,
gossiping about their dreary idols
and the vagaries of the Olympics in Atlanta.
Taken all together they do not have
the combined intellect of a lawn sprinkler.
We are watching a movie about the world's smartest man.
He is smart either because of extraterrestrial
aliens or because of a brain tumor.
The brain tumor is about to kill him
deader than the thought processes
of a House Republican even though he still
wants the woman he loves in spite
of the fact that she is the world's
meanest living human being
and even though she is mean most of all to him.
The best ideas of the world's smartest man
seem to involve improved methods
for using pig shit to power a car,
the arrangement of cars in a parking lot,
and the use of a photovoltaic cell to grow a zucchini.
He is not smart enough to be wary of the FBI,
to avoid the wrath of the local dull normals
and the assaults of the world's meanest woman.
The audience sobs at his pseudo pain,
chokes on their Snicker bars
and tries to grasp the concept of reading a book.
I sit in the dark munching stale popcorn
without butter flavoring
watching an actor who has had it made

since the moment of his birth
get paid fifteen million dollars to portray
pain and intellect to an audience
who barely has the intelligence to vote
itself into becoming the third world.
Now I will have to spend the rest
of the evening belching undigested popcorn
and line my coffin with
unpublished poems.

My Ears

Even though
my words flood
the seas of nonsense
and most men
multiply words
and starve to death
for want of
a single thought
my ears are
more useful
than my mouth.

Coming Home

7.10   Art is the conduit of value, the media of the
        psyche, the cultural barometer, the yoga of
        empathy, the healer of wounds, the ultimate free
        speech, the savior from madness, the data bank
        of the human condition, the conquest of apathy,
        the balm of hope, a compass for the lost, the
        keeper of love, the promise of joy and the
        revelation of epiphany.

7.10.1.9 You cannot read the same poem twice.

7.10.1.14 The poet is the practitioner of a dead art. A
        dead art is one in which the only audience is its
        practitioners. Even so poetry remains the last
        and only true art left in a free market culture, all
        others being reduced to artistic commodities.

7.10.1.29 Poetry is the yoga of empathy.

7.10.2 No market, free or otherwise, has the right or
        the means to value art.

7.10.2.0 In a free market the only good artist is a dead
        artist.

7.10.2.43 In a free market it is not possible, at the
        deepest level, to create art at all. It is only
        possible to create an artistic commodity.

We Had Everything

We had everything.

We died
to get nothing.

Do not trade trees for houses,
dreams for dollars
or mountains
for a city.

Do not trade your spirit
for pocketful of
change.

The Great Woolly Cloud Cat

I poked my head
out from the covers
and blew fog
into the air.
The fog
became
a great woolly
cloud cat.
The great woolly
cloud cat
curled up
on my chest,
licked my nose
with a tongue
of ice
and said —

"It's winter."

Waking, Summer

Drowsy summer morning.
I take my time waking up;
watch the dust swirl
in a spray of buttered sun.
From the moment time began
it has been too late.

Gardens

Some men believe
they can turn
a wilderness
into a garden,
forgetting
that wilderness is
the perfect garden.

A Walk In The Rain

At times we are the dreamer.
At times we are the dream.

A child's
head pressed
against the window pain.

Summer rain.

For The Dead

For the dead
there is always television
and sports and expensive meals,
cars, homes and children,
collecting butterflies or buttons
or useless, canceled stamps.

And for the dead
there is work and politics and war,
the annual vacation
and plumbing and poetry.

For the dead
must not be caught naked
on the cliffs of self,
must not lose track of his whereabouts
and fall into that black
pit of self
and wake up
one terrible morning
and find himself

alive.

Windows

The sky is aggressively cheerful
and I am in one of my moods again.
Open the shutters, I shout,
banging them wide,
and lean my forehead
against the glass.

The use of a window
is its emptiness.

No one, I am bellowing,
could want to close out the sky
on a day like this.

She sips her tea grumpily
and mutters, Who wants
to live in a fish bowl?

Tonight I am hiding from the storm.
It is trying to pry up my shingles
and drip into pots and pans.

All night a girl walks
up and down the street
in front of our house.
She is sobbing
in huge gasping gulps.
No one will ask her
what is wrong.
We are afraid that she is

stoned, or worse, crazy.

In the morning the girl is gone.
The storm is getting sleepy.

I look south,
beyond the window is a vastness,
the yawning jaws of death.

My hand is cupped on hot coffee, not sweet
but strong, a little of the sea
sluices through my heart, a little of the wind
howls in my lungs, a little rain
washes my vision, a little of the storm
rages in my mind.

Gross Assumptions

Birth.
Death.

In between
maybe 30000 trips to the toilet
and a few thousand half-hearted lays,
and lots and lots of tax.

That's all we know for sure.
And the rest —

gross assumptions.

Gnomae

10.8.3.4.17 If the species chooses stasis over quest and evolution, then the species is doomed. Life is evolution, death is static. The human adventure is here, down in the flux, the panta rhei, the change, the process and the evolution. Drugs have evolved by nature and by design. Some are good and some are bad. That's what humans have come equipped with brains for. There is risk.

10.8.3.4.18 It is, after all, the hero's quest.

Let The Worms Eat

Do not believe
that poets
sell you
their innermost
selves
when they
confess
every detail
even though
they will tell you
every other truth
and any truth you ask.
Bury me
in a shallow grave
and let the worms
eat my brain.
They will learn
nothing
of value.

Devotee Of The Inconsequential

A poet
is a bandit,
a thief of minds,
at home in the night,
spreading disorder,
urinating on convention,
walking on the grass,
breaking limits,
sneaking over the border,
practitioner of the random,
devotee of the
inconsequential
and there is no one else
who will tell you
the truth
and no one else
who could care less.

Meeting Gods

Walk any road
and meet gods
tramping between
better worlds.
Most gods,
no matter how useless,
began their travels
in the geography
of some man's mind
and although
most men
never meet their gods
on either a road
or in a thought
the best men
meet gods in both
and even though
some men
will take the time
to free a god
from immortality
I walk on
and forget
them all.

Going To Bed

I turn out the lights,
curl up beneath the covers
and all my ghosts
climb into bed
beside me.
My ghosts guard
my sleep,
drink my tears,
inhabit my dreams
and in the morning
the sun scatters
my ghosts into the dawn
and in my eyes
the sun can find only
deserts of talc.

The Goodyear Blimp

It hovers over our houses
our beach, our streets
and the privacy of my backyard.
A whale of a peeping tom,
bobbing along the sky —
a great disembodied penis.

Tonight the blimp will light up
and interrupt my dreams with
advertisements for Coors beer
horny nineteen year old girls
and someone else's good life.

We do not have all the time in the world,
so every dream must count.

We are in love, so
we hold hands in the agony of the dusk.

The sun rattles it's death,
magenta and gold.

Night.

The Place
Where I Will Die

13.9.4 The male sex has been manipulated into the
services of the elite by replacing traditional
initiation systems with war. The primary myth
that a boy can only become a man by killing
another boy trying to become a man has nearly
brought the species to the brink of annihilation.

13.9.5 The female primary myth that only by spawning
can a girl become a woman has had even more
catastrophic impact on humanity.
Overpopulation remains one of the prime
motivations for war.

13.9.6 The girls make them, the boys kill them. It is
free market equilibrium in practice.

In A Crack Of Rock

Morning mist
hides the mountain.

Below me,
the forest.

Here, the stream
plunges, anxious
and ignorant
to the sea.

The pine
tries to catch
the wind.

Drifting cloud.

A far off
mountain
is like a woman.

A few flowers
dying
in a crack of rock.

Twilight

The mountain
solitary
and huge
sponges up
the twilight.

The valley
fills with
wood smoke
and shadow.

I lay back
against
smooth granite
and watch.

Not a thing
crosses
my mind.

In Return

Stars
sprayed on
the forest roof,
run away
into nothing.

Our campfire
spits embers,
trying to catch
the stars.

They fall
black and cold
to the earth.

This small
green ball
circles its star,
screaming with life,
as though
all is well.

The campfire,
the frogs,
the crickets
and the stream
call the stars,
"Come back.
We love you."

In return,
we hear only
a vast,
irrational
silence.

Jackass Lake

1
Up the mountain
follow the stream
pine and fir
a stone silence
some wind, and
a green silence.

Beside a fallen pine
rotting into soil
a blood red snow flower
breaks earth
pulling down the sky.

2
Up the mountain
follow the stream
the granite valley
sweat and dust and stone
summer storm
brewing hot clouds.

Rest by the stream
a cool drink
soak your feet
soak your shirt
soak your head.

3
A quiet day
a silent heat
green mountain lake
in a granite teacup.

Swimming
naked as a stone.

Just Before Bed

The clouds swirl —
no hurry,
elegant with sloth.

Fog drifts
through the brick canyons
the same way London goes to bed.

The moon is a fuzzy peach.
It falls, rotten
with promise.

Only the roar of the rapid
keeps me from hearing
the chatter of the stars.

For an hour
I watch coals
mourn the death
of flame.

Snow

It's fall.
It's water.
It's rain.
It's fog.

It's moss so green
my eyes see purple
when I look at clouds.

It's wet nettles.

It's the smell of resin
and turpentine.

It's dead quiet.
It's no dust.
It's no acid-blue sky.
It's a red twilight.
It's mushrooms under a log.
It's busy chipmunks.
It's bluejays not scolding.

It's the forest
and it's the mountain.

It's waiting for the snow.

An Event In Autumn

A leaf falls,
the earth shakes.

I watch a spider
crawl into the fire.

The leaf flies
back into the tree.

Gravestones

Stumps only,
the gravestones
of sequoias.

Seeing this great life
only a man
could cut it down.

When the stars
have forgotten
our names

who will plant flowers
on our graves
when there are no trees
to weep for us.

A Dream Of Stones

I will remember the pine, solemn
and dancing, drunk with the wind
and the ticking of the seasons.
I will remember the mountains,
the stones, granite and obsidian,
the wind, a few insects, hawks and eagles.

Death is the topography of our dreams.

And when the sun explodes
voracious for a dark sleep,
and the earth is burned clean
of oceans and trees and hawks
perhaps the mountains, perhaps the stone
in their long, dark dreaming
will recall the setting sun
the falling snow,
the wind,
the pine,

and me.

Walking Stick

I found a stick.
It fit my hand.
It was the right length.
I smacked it over a rock
because it was cottonwood,
but it held
so I shaped it with the broad axe,
finished it with my knife,
oiled it with corn oil
and let it bake in the sun.
I bound a hand grip
with eighth inch nylon
and burned the knots,
leaned it against the rock
by my shoes
waiting for my blisters
to let me take a walk.

When you walk
one mile or a thousand
keep your eyes on the horizon
and keep your feet on the ground.
You put the stick
where you don't want to put your feet
until you know
exactly
where
you are stepping.

A Cup Of Thunder

Mist so thick
I am lost in a
forest of five trees.

Rain so hard
I can't hear my feet
crushing nettles and twigs.

Clouds so thick
the mountain puts on
its gray sweatshirt.

The forest shivers,
shaking rain from its fur.

The fog turns the forest
from a cathedral
to a cave.

The world gets smaller
all the time,
and more private
and what I know best
is a few stones,
a Druid's circle
of trees and rain
and sometimes
a quiet so loud
it turns my ear
into a cup of thunder.

Branch And Twig

You need
a strong branch
for walking.

For contemplation,
a small twig

to draw hieroglyphs
in the sand.

Clouds

Storm black —

dusk wind
tearing dust
and trash.

Sky —
solemn ink
a floating mountain
a sky cathedral

chasing wind

bringing rain.

For The Old Man

East Fork Of The Portuguese Creek, High Sierras

This is home.
This mountain
these rock balls
this stream and sky and cloud
these trees.

Since I was a boy
I've known the faces of these stones,
their crystal dreams of the sea
these fingers of pine and toes of fir —
listened to their long rootless dreams
traded news and songs
with the afternoon wind
chattered with the creek
local gossip, past storms, hard winters.
The deer and squirrels
aren't around much anymore
but the mountain is old
and remembers who I am.

This mountain is my spirit of place.
It is where I am
in the geography of things.
It is where I bring those
I want to share my self with.
It is where my mind
dances its dreams of meaning.
It is where I will die
no matter where I die.

And death for me
is never to hike above the horizon
and see this lake again.
It is never to sit in a deep quiet
and hear the wind and fir again.
It is never to awake in the dawn
with the sun looking for my eyes
over the hill and through the trees
again.

And death for me is to become the place.
This geometry of stone and pine
will recall my dreams
this harmonics of wind and creek
will sing my name,
this immense mountain
will remember who I am.

The old man gave me many things
birth and money and education.
The old man gave me a way
of looking at things,
bicycles for Christmas
and poor eyesight.
The old man gave me good times
and hard times
and a sense of dignity.

And more than all the rest
my old man
gave me this mountain.

Gnomae

13.11.2 It is the genius of love to leap that horizon of
unknowing and embrace another mind. It is love
to acknowledge freedom.

Longer Than A Fruit Fly

The streets crawl
with tax paying
consumers,
lungs pumping
sour smog
and although
most men
pretend
to be alive
longer
than a dead fruit fly
the truth is
that very few men
are actually
alive enough
to know
the difference.

Rather Die

No one dies
who has never thought
and although
no one thinks
who has not
looked into
the eyes of death
most men
would rather die
than think.

The Economic Cog

I was born standing flat on both feet.
I do not mean to imply that I have a life.
I am a born wage slave and a beast of burden.
I left my knee prints at the feet of the glass cathedrals of
        commerce.
One day I ate steamed vegetables for lunch.
That afternoon I was old.
This year love is an unfunded mandate.
I am the single burnt neuron in the network.
It is better to live life than to celebrate it.
I never sold a dream for a dollar.
They/god/it/life killed every dream in my jungle.
Profit is the shovel that digs my grave.
Employment is the lumber of my coffin.
There is no greater waste of a human mind.
I am an economic cog now.
I work. I consume.
I let basketball stars tell me what to think.
I expect a gold watch and a cremation at public expense.
I paid my taxes.
I never would have guessed that life could be so short.

And A Good Day

So I went out
and fired up the car
and everything was smooth
and I went to the market
and I got everything I wanted
and the checkline had no line
and I had money in my account
and I drove home singing
and the traffic parted way
and all the signals were green
and I was happy
and I was in control
and I smiled at the people
and the people smiled at me
and I had the world wired.

One Of Those Days

When the alarm exploded at four I dreamed
that my head was smoking from electroshock
and I threw my legs over the bed
fighting the wave of nausea in my stomach
and I knew that this was going to be
one of those days that they call 'one of those days.'
Three steps down the hallway a very wet
hairball squished up between my toes.
I went to the kitchen and burned my lamb burger.
I forgot the honey in my coffee and then
I remembered that I forgot the anti-biotic pill.
I lost every game of solitaire on the computer
so I knew that fate had it in for me today.
I ran out of time so I jumped into the shower
grateful that Samantha the cat had abandoned
her new spot on the sink. I dropped the soap
six times in the tub and when I turned off the water
I remembered that I forgot to wash my hair
so I turned it back on and scalded my nose.
Samantha pranced in and screamed at me for daring
to remove the towel that padded her spot on the sink
so I leaned out of the tub to retrieve her towel
and smashed my toe on the tub.
I was late getting out the door so I was in trouble
traffic wise, but by the time I hit Marine
I shit my pants because of the anti-biotics
and because I forgot to spend a precautionary
moment on the toilet before I left.
Someone else cut off an angry blond in a BMW
so she cut me off causing me to hit the brakes

so hard I almost broke into a skid
and then she turned around with the scowl of Medusa
and flipped me the finger. I smiled and flipped it back.
On the connecting ramp to the 105
an angry black woman cut me off when her lane ended
and I hit the brakes in time to avoid scraping
down the cement wall. A mile further on
she tried to cut me off again in the slow lane
but when I didn't let her she flipped me the finger
and blew her horn. I smiled and flipped it back.
I made it to work and charged upstairs to the toilet
just in time to evacuate an emergency explosion
of anti-biotic diarrhea. I washed my underwear,
and my ass, padded both dry with paper towels
and went back to the truck to lay down for
fifteen minutes before the day began for real.
When we all occupy our respective cubicles
we discover that the upstairs keys are missing.
Bad karma, it seems, is not restricted to the individual.
By ten I walk over to Pasqua for a caffeine fix.
I notice that my toe hurts more than it should.
I guess I broke it. All that matters now is my coffee.
Coming out of the shop I am attacked by an angry
street woman who demands that I hand over my change
which, normally, I would, but I didn't have any
and she wasn't going to allow me to get away with that.
She wants to debate the issue with me.
I explain to her that I am old, tired and in pain.
My femur is broken, the scafoid is cracked
and my ankle is destroyed. I no longer have
a right latissimus, my adrenals are shot,
my immune system went south, my endocrines are
        dysfunctional,

my leg hurts, my head throbs, and my back aches.
My toe is broken, my heart is shattered, my liver
gives me the sweats, I have an infection in my graft,
and diarrhea from the antibiotics, a pressure ulcer
on my heal and all my dreams are broken.
I am in debt to Master Card for twenty grand,
I have no pension, no security and no savings.
No one publishes me, no reads me and no is ever likely
      to.
"Catch me tomorrow," I smile. "And have a nice day"

I grit my teeth and limp across Normandy
anticipating the rest of the day.

So much for the easy part.

The Mullah
And The Pusher

13.12.11 A living child has greater rights than the
unborn.

13.12.12 40,000 children died today of starvation or
malnutrition.

13.12.13 As long as a single child starves anywhere on
the planet, no one has the ethical justification to
produce another child.

My Own Way

Dallas, Texas

A gravel path
beside a winter-dead field
leads back to the concrete block hotel,
and the plastic rooms
and the charged nylon carpet
and the synthetic sheets
and the foam pillow
and the TV
and I trudge along
until a single footprint
blocks my path
and I get off the one-way path
and walk back
on the winter-dead grass
in the winter-dead field
and make my own way.

Somewhere Over France

Below —

a sea of cloud
curiously immobile

a serene ocean
of charcoal currents

chalk waves
that never crest

and alabaster tides
frozen in the
silence of form

sculpted above
the volatile gas
of human aspirations,

the waste dumps
of human doings,

the fetid swamps
of human dreams

the clouds prefer
to reflect the stars.

Stone In Flight

Tehran

Autumn,
the days, still hot—
among the mountains
only Damavand
carries snow,
the white agony
of stone in flight,
it arches into
the acid-blue
freedom of the sky.

Sky blind
a drifting cloud
brings a season
and seasons
measure the dance
of drunken planets.

I grow old, not wise.
It is autumn now,
the days are still hot
and among men
only I am snow bound.

The seasons
tick madly away,
a clock
wound too tight.

Crows Flying Around Hoseinieh Ershad

Davoudieh, Tehran

Crows have it,
wisdom,
buzzing around the sky
cawing and shitting.

I sit in my kitchen,
three stories up
as high as any crow on a wire.

They sit on a naked tree
and telephone wires
staring in my window,
smug.

They are amazed
that I have no wings.

I sip my tea and stare back,
trying to look like a member
of an intelligent species,

trying to figure out
what they know

that I don't.

Hard Times

Tehran

Runes in smoke,
cancerous in the air,
things go on
the way things have gone before.

A dog dies — love.
The pointless brutality of things — love.
Leaves torn from limb — love.
The bill arrives,
too much for too little — love.
Days passing
in the grim mills of whim — love.
I follow what comes
and don't give a damn.

Love.

A Day's Trivia

Tehran

The angry insistence
of cars and bosses
and brain dead landlords
drags me out of bed.

The sun is laughing,
bright, and the sky
fierce with clarity.

I crawl to work,
negotiate a day's trivia.

In the sky, cruel blue
and pale white, the moon
is dying,
the sun is
busy
elsewhere.

Dawn, Tehran

No one asked
the day to break.

The poor, dead quiet,
shuffle through the dust.

In the center
of the highway
a sunflower
faces the sun.

The moon,
cloud white,
bobs above
Mt. Damavand.

Life is for the ignorant.

We call it innocence
and eventually

knowledge kills us.

Street Sweepers, Tehran

The silent wisdom of the opium smile
dreamlike
the sweepers dust the asphalt
shoes without soles
frayed suit coats
unwashed all winter long
stroking with twig brooms
endlessly
the gravel, the litter, the dust
returns tomorrow
brushed into the gutters
dreamlike
returns
the sweepers
in the silent wisdom of the opium smile
stroking
worlds, far off
in dreams of smoke.

Things Go On

Sitting in bars of light,
the morning sun
burns through the blind,
and the tea kettle,
steaming like winter time
fogs the windows.

And me —
sitting around
thinking grand ultimate thoughts,
solving great riddles,
formulating astounding poems
creating the lies of history
and every thought I ever had,
every word I ever wrote —
ignored.

The sun rises.
The pot steams.
Windows fog.
Things go on.

Treadmills

Tehran

I step into the street.
The earth rolls beneath my feet.
I step along the ground
and the city treadmills.
I am a rat scrambling
on the outside of the treadmill
and I look up at the sun
and notice that I never move
and the asphalt
just spins by below
and time spirals
down the gutter's drain.

Muscle Under Grace

She is a young girl,
about ten, faded Levis
flaring over tennis shoes
and wearing a boy's plaid shirt.

We are in a hell called Iran.
She is young and blond and female
and a foreigner in a land
that hates all of the above.

She toes the dirt, pensively,

suddenly breaking into a run —
the long liquid stride,
animal power, joyous muscle
dancing in the grace of the sun.

Perfect symmetry,
her long, bright hair
dancing in the wind.

She is spirit over gravity.
I am a thirty year old man
stretching out aching muscles.
I know how the tug of the earth,
the suck of mud,
eats spirit in the end.

She flares
brighter than all the planets,

all their deadly pull,
brighter than all their
hungry suns.

I am clay
melting into mud.

The earth
cannot grab
her feet.

Out Of Phase, Tehran

They ooze through the veins of the bazaar
like those old school day cartoons
of white corpuscles
carrying out the evil germs.

Men that do nothing their whole lives
but carry the load—
carpets and pots and pans,
dead goats, samovars, crates of rice,
their shoulders heaved to the ground,
backs forever bent
into a parody of right angles.

I am walking beside a hunchback porter.
Our views of things are 90 degrees out of phase.
His eyes never leave the ground.
Mine never leave the horizon.

I go everywhere, tripping and falling.
He goes nowhere,

                    and never stumbles.

The Key Man, South Tehran

The key man is filing
and dancing before the vise.
He is hacking a key
from a block of brass.

Bandy legs and gray hair,
ear to ear smiles,
serious concentration —
he dances out to the bike
trying each key
again and again.

Two and a half hours
for six keys,
another hour for fine tuning.

He doesn't quit
till he makes it perfect.

I think about a machine
that does it good enough
in a minute flat.

When I pay him,
he is 27 feet of smiles,
happy as a pipe full of kif.

I never met a machine
that was happy in its work.

Tehran Nightmare

Yesterday
the snow
fell like it didn't want
to touch the earth.

And when it did,
things being the way they are,
it turned to mud
and that's a hell of a come down
for a snow flake
and a bad dream for sure.

About that time
I woke up,
rattling with cold
and sure enough,
my economy minded landlady
had turned off the heat.
I knew it was useless
to go down and make a scene,
things being the way they are.

So I fell into a frozen sleep
and dreamed
that I was a snowflake
and I wake up in the morning
and look at the mud

and think better of it.

Imaginary Sun

Outside the winter window,
the rain flushes sewers of garbage,
wild dogs eat children on the street,
ten year old boys become the sex slaves
of construction gangs
and some infantile god grumbles,
his dreams rattle in their cages.
In his sleep
he fondles an erection
and a few men are born and a few die
and the world revolves an imaginary sun.

So Many Steps, A Mountain

So many steps
to climb a mountain.

The snow
can't quite make up its mind.
Berserk Iranians
are running downhill
with blaring radios.
They are wearing
leather soled street shoes,
galloping down the ice.

At last, high enough,
silence and snow
flirting in the fog.

Alone
in the cold
with the music
of water.

Beggars

Some beg because they hate.
Some beg because they are lazy.
Some beg because they need.
Most beg because there is no choice.

That any man begs
is the degradation of every man.
And any man that begs,
needs.

No man fills up his needs
and we all die
devouring one another
in a daisy chain
of stomachs.

The Art Of Love

Ponds of water,
gravel roads,
sundeath —

I fall into cracks in the pavement,
submerge into dying flowers,
the perfect symmetry
of cloud and sky,
a mule and a man
swirl in dust and distance.

A Tehran Love Poem

So
times are tough
and the workmen next door
punk this kid, which was okay
but the kid cries all night
from so much attention.

So
upright citizens make a call
and the old man comes down
kicking ass and taking names
and the kid, I guess,
cries from hunger now —

and so.

Born Artists
12 Jan 74, Tehran

We are born artists
and philosophers
and after a few years
death is
a paranoid's dream —

so little left
to kill.

My Death

Someone hushed up
the sun —
I have lived, died and
I gave it everything I had —
autumn in Tehran,
dust and traffic —
loving you
my life shines
in the tar soup of life —
a bare room,
two people get up,
talking,
cross the room,
go out the door
and the room
is empty, dead quiet
and the door shuts,
clicks into place,
and it's that simple —

my death.

Cats, Sun, Myself

Before the sun
and the defecations of the tourists,
I was the first into the Acropolis.

Athens is quiet that moment before
the sun claws its way over the horizon.
There are only a few cats, a few birds
the sun, my self
and this bright,
unbearable
beauty.

Gnomae

13.24   The soul may be a human artifact.

Toes To Eyes

I have
four limbs, a head
and walk upright.
I am not worth this mornings
overcooked eggs
and burnt potatoes.
There is nothing
behind these sore eyes
to justify getting
out of bed.
Here I am, facing
myself in the mirror.
Not a pretty sight.
Nothing but an unhappy
pottage of mass
and bad habits
glues these toes
to these eyes into
this kind of idiot.

Time to shave.

Becoming A Man

Boys who think that
boys become men
by killing other boys
trying to become men
never become man enough
to admit that no boy
becomes a man
until he has been
destroyed
by a woman.

The Only Luck

Indite the stars
for conspiracy.
The pundits threaten
a quiet evening.
Simple birth guarantees
bad luck.
The only duty of one who knows
is to get out of bed,
work hard,
eat little,
love much
and save a slice of bread
as if there is no fate
but one's own
passing dream,
the only luck
the smile
of a
child.

Fook Gins

I am sitting in Fook Gins
eating Pork Won Ton,
watching the cars go by,
clouds go by, days go by
and I am thinking about
poems that have no end
that fade into night
the way daylight fades
into a foggy dusk.

No use trying to taste
everything on the menu,
to look into or out of
those millions of windows
crowding these endless streets,
or count all those clouds
sailing on the window pane.

It's better to taste
a few things well.

For me, it's Pork Won Ton
just as the day fades into fog
and a single cloud, painted
on a window pane
puts the sun to sleep.

Master/Slaves

A slave
is anyone
without a voice
and although
the master class
has stolen
the power
to express
one's self
they die
without
a self to
express.

Machu Picchu

16.1　One free lunch is the problem with every
　　　explanation of final or ultimate causes.

Daisies On Moyoc Marca

The Round Fortress Of Sacsahuaman

It circles fire.
The sun circles stone,
the dawn
pointing to a season
of corn and sacrifices.

The circle points everywhere.

The stone gutters
drink blood and corn beer.
Stars were born in this rock,
hearts ripped and daisies took root.
A thousand Incas died here
of a disease called conquest.
The Inca ruled over the sun festival
and over the four directions,
four quarters in a circle
and the circle points
everywhere.

A storm pours light
down the mountain.
Cusco is a bowl
of melted butter.
The rain circles
clouds, chasing the sun,
stars are born in the rock,
daisies take root
in the blood.

Walking down the mountain
it rains.

A Stone Wall

Sacsahuaman

The Imperial Falcon

A year to quarry a stone.
A year to move it.
A year to carve it.
A year to lift it into place just so.
Just so each stone,
a maze of planes and angles,
no mortar,
just men and stone,
llamas and rawhide ropes,
dirt banks and clay models.
So many stones ground to dust.
So many men ground to paste.
Stones,
the Incas said,
were once
men.

I photograph a wall.
The bottom course of stone
half again as tall as a man.
The air is electric with calm,
wind bitten,
cold and clean.
The storm is rolling over the mountain,
clouds boiling up the hill
down into Cusco,
blue steel,
lead,

silver,
and fat with rain.

The stones watch
as calm as the mountain,
still as snow.

Every stone
is a cloud at heart.

Huaynpicchu

Machu Picchu

The place where the sun is fastened is below me,
fixed in granite, chained to minds.
I look back, hide my pack behind a bush and climb the
      mountain.

The city is below me, a geometry of stone
eaten by rain and the ticking of the wind.

A ladder of granite is chiseled in the mountain.
Its stone face winces with pain.
I climb straight up.
It is slimy with water and moss,
the way I get dizzy with height,
the suck of the earth tugging at my heels.

I am strapped to the sun.

The condor breaks stone beneath the prison floor,
flexes wings, feathers light as light,
sheer, spiraling past the temple of the moon
where snakes are wise with the mysteries of women.
This stone peak, wedged into the sky by the hammers of
      men.
The sky is raining blue glass.
These clouds drifting by waist high.

This is as high as men go.

The condor soars beyond the sky's cracked skull,

spirals again, piercing clouds —
the sun, the sun, the sun.

It is not that the many worlds are false —
only the city's vast death of dust and weeds
and the enthusiasm of the jungle,
the wind, feathers ruffled, gliding slow, circles
around, around, around

the sun.

Below me I see little men.
Their cities are oil spread on a mud pond.
Their groans of war and famine and jails and the rich
and all their screams and sighs of passion
drift up in the whimper of a bamboo flute.

The gush of the wind makes a finer tune.

My eye is white fire.
I am the condor,
wings, feathers, wind — soar higher.
Clouds, mountains, cold — glide higher.
Oceans, horizons, storms — fly higher, higher, higher.
Air, vast sky
sun, sun, sun, sun, sun —

so many stars.
It is not that the many worlds are false
only that each world is chained
to a different sun.

Whatever Goes Up

You go that high
and it brings you down,
the suck of men,
the suck that keeps stones from flying,
keeps mountains rooted to the earth,
rivers flushing carrion to the sea.
It pulls you down every day,
the women,
the jobs,
that river of debts,
holes in the socks,
flat tires,
good music,
good times,
good food,
that sea of fire the stomach,
"Feed me or die."
Raving up here on your mountain
you can't eat air and sunlight,
flying in clouds and rainbows
your feet know where to go,
down.
Down to that sense of earth
that swallows us whole.

Two tourists from Britain
climb like goats for 45 minutes,
take three breaths
and four cardinal photographs,
"Got to go. Got to go. Got to go,"

they run down the mountain
photographing everything,
seeing nothing —
no sky,
no sun,
no clouds,
no city laying like a stone maze
just beneath the clouds,
no stone condor flying to the sun.
They see only a split image in a black box.

A few years from now
they will build a cable car
up Huaynpicchu
and a snack bar at the top
They will cover the whole city
with a plumber's nightmare
of catwalks and guided tours.
They will eat tossed green tourist dollars.
They will build asphalt rivers.
They will print tickets and menus.
The clouds will freeze and turn to stone,
hide the sun in a cold cave.
The condor will circle
down to its stone prison
under the jail,
fold its wings
and petrify.

It is a paradox,
this boundary
that pins here to now.
If you can stomach the vision

the moment is yours.

Take it.

Your feet know where to go
when your eyes are blind
with the sun —
down, down, down
into the subterranean terror
of our day to day life.

You have no choice.

When you go this high
any direction at all
and every path you take
is down.

Portrait

The sun is sliding down the sky.
The sea stretches wide
its dark, gray womb.

A single flower
stands in the window.

The sun paints its shadow
on the wall.

Night.

The Dancer, Cusco

It is late Sunday afternoon.
There isn't much doing,
sun,
clouds,
children,
the usual.

Over by the colonnade
a crowd is watching
a one man band.
He is dressed in rags,
worn out sandals
and a mechanics rag
tied around his head.
His face has the intense look
of a moron.

He plays just three notes
on a harmonica,
in a crude tune,
over and over and over
and he dances forward six steps
and hits a 5 gallon can
hanging from his neck.
Then he does the same thing backwards.

He does this 417 times
before I go away.
The crowd loves him.
They clap in time

with his three notes
and one bang.

There is a simpleton dancing
in the gut and skull
of every man, god and galaxy.

This simpleton dances in Cusco
on Sunday afternoons
for anybody's
nickel.

The guidebooks do not mention him.

For 2 Cents

10,000 hard days
plowed up his forehead.
30,000 skimpy meals
pocked craters
in his cheeks.
He is sleeping
on the steps
of the Cusco train station,
folded like yesterday's
newspaper into
each 90 degrees.
3,000 days of grime
ground his clothes
to a loose
collection of strings.

He could not
have touched a woman
for 30 years.

He has a sack
of cocaine leaves
to chew when
his stomach begins
to digest his spine.

He catches me
taking his picture
in his tourist pose,
screams about
stealing his soul
and in the end
I have to buy it
for 2 cents.

Children, Plaza De Armas

Cusco

The sun rolls over the mountain.
The park bench turns to ice.
It's Sunday.
I am the only one left
except for Jesus up on the hill.

The flies are gone.
The beggars are gone.
Even the shoeshine boys have left me alone.

Tomorrow I am going to Machu Picchu
looking for the same old answers.
But they're the wrong questions and it's the wrong place
and what do stones and mountains know anyway.

A bunch of children come into the plaza.
I am the only toy in sight.

They stand in a circle and watch me write
until they can't stand it anymore—
Senor, in Ingles, que dice?

In English this is a pen
this is paper
this is a watch
and what you have just tugged on is a beard.

They are laughing like the sun never sets
like there are no dead civilizations

like there is no cement Jesus.
Children don't ask the wrong questions.

This is a jacket.
This is my ear.
This is a love poem.

I am giving it to you.

Hands And Peas
Cusco Market

Hands and peas
potatoes and carrots
soles and fingers
this for that
everyone is trading
pork chops for bananas
and everyone's
a cheater.

This for that
a shirt for a hammer
a hammer for potatoes
potatoes for a knife
a knife for a trout
a trout for a backrub
a backrub for a washing machine
a washing machine
will get you laid
and getting laid is like a potato.

Altaplana

So high it gets dizzy
Lake Titicaca hangs in the sky.

It never drips.

Like clouds,
it's huge
and barren as
a bath without bubbles—
endless dust,
endless mud,
endless gravel,
a few mud baked houses.
The rich have tin
roofs and locks on the door.

The thieves all have rusted
fingers and empty eye sockets.

The donkeys all sweat flies.

And the flies have got it
good.

Faces Of Tiahuanaco

Someone no one knows
carved these faces
into white rock.

No one knows the
faces either.

Tiahuanaco had an empire.
It didn't last.
They just were not mean enough.

These faces
look too smart to be
generals and merchants.

That's why they are hanging
on this wall
in a pit
in La Paz,
staring at another wall
that has no
faces at all.

Gnomae

16.3.10 Reality is a game for two or more players.

Life Is Dukha

Every day I am becoming Buddha.
I can't seem to stop it.
Soon I expect to be as bald as a summer squash.
I am growing a respectable pot belly.
I am down to three grains of rice a day.
My arms will turn to sticks.
I am beginning to smile as if I knew secrets.
My hands keep making funny gestures.
My eyelids seem to be getting fatter
and they are almost always shut.
I talk in riddles that don't even make sense to me.

I don't get it.
I used to be a comer.
I got old instead.
I used to be a poet.
The world had other ideas.
I used to make money.
Now I'm looking for refrigerator boxes
and staking out freeway underpasses.
I used to have things on my mind
but life took my voice away.

The universe keeps bringing things to my doorstep.
And the universe keeps taking things away.
I never had a chance.
I guess I never will.

Be careful what you want.

If you want it bad, you'll get it bad.
Buddha said that desire is the root of all pain.
Learn to live without wants he said.
He called this sage advice.

I call it learning to live
with lowered expectations.

Holy shit! my ears are growing down to my shoulders.
I am beginning to stink like a man
who wears cheap serenity for cologne.

I am beginning to attract disciples
like a compost pile attracts flies.

Life is deprivation and ecstasy.
Life ignored my art and strangled my thought.
Life is a series of broken dreams interrupted by death.
I made no difference and I will die without a voice.
Life wasted me.

I have never been so glad to be alive.

I hate the stench of wisdom in the morning.
The price for understanding is everything you've got.
Just about the time you figure life out it's gone.
The deepest realization is the most profound ignorance.
The more I know the less I understand.
God save me from one more revelation.

Hell, now I can't get a hard on anymore.
I have finally learned to live without love.
It's a matter of spiritual triage, a matter of lobotomy.

I see a beautiful woman these days and I just get tired.

I can't seem to get rid of this god damned golden aura.
My legs are frozen in the lotus position.

It turns out that
the best cure for a headache
is the guillotine.

A Hungry Mind

Life's only consistent nourishment
is a diet of chronic bad luck
and the only way to lose life
and clench it tight in the fist
is to choose not to surrender
to despair knowing that
the only weapon bad luck fears
is a hungry mind.

Forks In The Road

When the tyrant first appears
he is a protector.
Suspect the country
that has no death.
Kill every executioner.
Rebel against perfection.
Pursue risk.
Seek diversity.
Choose always
the path
that leads
to other
paths.

The Secret Of Death

Pain alone
exposes
the secret
of death
and knowing pain
is the secret
to sharing
a private
joke
with
death.

Surprised

To live forever
is to be perpetually
surprised
and although
most men
die of mental
deprivation
the only one
that one must
surprise
is one's
self.

RiverRun

16.5.14 To make one another real is an act of grace.

16.5.21.3 Love alone redeems us. The lover, the
empathic person always derives the greatest
good, the reality of self in the sudden and
awesome illumination that the primal terror
holds no threat; we are not alone in spite of the
fact that we have no certainty.

16.5.22 It is the act of empathy to leap the horizon of
uncertainty again and again. Love is our talent.
Empathy is our act of grace.

Desert Quiet

Not many things are this quiet,
snow maybe,
or heat
and many words.
The air is white iron.
The sky is blue steel.
I am in the canyon by a pool
more quiet than snow,
more still than rock.

It is twenty feet across,
three feet deep,
clear and the bottom so green
it turns black in the shadow.

A sandstone mesa,
a cloud
and some sky
are floating on the water.
A cottonwood for shade,
the earth blisters mud and lava,
and nothing moves;
not the water,
not the air,
not the fantastic dance of stone.

When I want to build the world
in a different way

I go to the desert alone.
It is between me and the world
to make things the way we agree,
not a single voice
to keep me sane,
not a single word
to make me see sense.

Nothing moves;
not the wind,
not me.
Zeno saw it —
this bellybutton in a merry-go-round,
a billion suns
revolving this silence.

After a while it cools off.
I hear a pattern in the sounds.
Silence is the glue
between each note;
a fly heading north,
a bird calling far up the canyon,
the wind gushing through the cottonwood,
the way I swing a stick swooshing through the air.

My heart jerking like an epileptic
the flutter of dragonflies
jousting above the pond —
all
my

life
comes down to this canyon
quiet as snow,
quiet as heat,

quiet as the death
of old men.

Through The Goosenecks

The river is a sentence of Ss.
It winds through the goosenecks.
It winds to the left.
It winds right.
It winds in loops.
It winds around castles.
It winds through cliffs.
It winds through stones.
It winds around sand bars.
It winds around canyons.
It winds over old shoes.
It winds slow.
It winds fast.
It winds up dead in Lake Powell,
oil and garbage and water skiers
where water is only water.
It winds up as night rain
splashing light all over this page.
It winds up in a radiator.
It winds up in a coca cola.
It winds up in a toilet bowl,
a cheerful and sanitary blue.
It winds up taking rings out of collars.
It winds up in a sewer.
It winds up in the sea
for fish to fuck in.

The river chuckles in the rapid.
I am laughing in the sun.
We do not have all the time in the world.
We are glad to be alive.

Time To Kill

1

You've got to have time —
time to wait for storms,
time to wait them out.

Dollars don't buy it.
I can't sell it to you.
I can't give it to you
in this poem,
or in pictures,
or in a thousand other storms,
in a thousand other lives.
Years won't give you time —
this time,
this river.

2

The shutter bangs across.
I picture him that way,
his back towards me,
his knee lifted high
climbing the waterfall —
my brother,
forever
stepping toward the sun.

4

The juniper,

older than the knuckles
of the oldest man,
more green
than rotten cheese,
more gnarled
than the life of a bureaucrat,
its roots still clutch the stone,
the parched earth —
roots ripped, naked
from the ground,
limbs reaching
for the sun,
pulling down the sky.

6
Spitting steel and thunder
the waterfall,
the sun
splashing over the rock,
streams of fire —

we are naked
under the fall,
laughing.

I am taking a picture
of the way things stand.
I open the aperture
to get more light,
and the thunder
grows louder.

8

We get on our boots and clothes,
head down to the bleeding river.
The heat eats wormholes in my head.
My skin is a baking wasteland,
dried mud cracked and curling
with little acid rivers of sweat and salt.
My legs keep me from the fate of stones.

Evening storm
hovers in an ocean of fading sun.
The clouds
chase us down
the gulch.

Riverrat Macho

I sit with my feet
soaking in the river.

Grind my blade
on a soft ouchita stone,
then an Arkansas hard
and a few last strokes
on a surgical black.

I run the knife
down my arm.
The hairs fall
like snow.

There are those
who will judge you
by the sharpness
of your blade.

Suncat

Last night it was
clouds and wind
and cold enough
to wear a shirt.

This morning
it's a Kodachrome sky.

The sun is melting
the goose pimples on my back.

It bounces off the river,
projects
up under an overhanging shelf,
prowling and purring
it licks the stone with flame.

Maps And Metaphors

Mexican Hat, San Juan River

I climbed the canyon wall,
stone so hot
it boiled blisters
on my fingers.

Three false trails,
only one worth a damn,
gets me to the top.
It should only be a quarter mile to the road.
I guess on the direction by the sun and the river.
Half way down the road
in a litter of beer cans
and 1940 automobiles
I find a map that some
lost soul threw away.

This map
was not even the wrong territory.
It's Alabama,
a place I never intend to go
since my grandmother died a baptist
and a racist.

I walk down the littered highway.
Words don't get you around the bend.
Your feet do.

It's a god damn steep hill back to camp
with 40 pounds of food

and a half gallon of cold milk.
I watch the cars drive through the asphalt
like it was hot black butter.
I'm going to try to get a ride.

If we didn't have fingers
and a thumb,
god,
we'd all be some kind
of metaphor.

Purple

Changed my mind
with a little purple pill.
Came out of the shade,
sat down in the river
watching things go by
with a permanent grin
cracking my jaw.

A dragonfly lands on my shoulder.
Everything about him is purple,
purple wings,
purple legs,
purple feelers,
a zillion purple eyes
and big fuzzy purple jaws —
no hint of a smile —
opening and closing,
munching on the idea
of me for lunch.
And I could see down that purple throat
to the purple pit of his stomach
waiting for me.
But when I laughed
he buzzed off
and I dove under
and came up
cold.

The Little Ones Never Get Away

It's early.

The sun
is pussyfooting
around
in black clouds.

I am up alone,
gather some firewood,
stoke up the coals.

A two inch catfish
is trapped in a bucket of drinking water,
swimming in circles,
looking for
a river.

The Red Menace

My feet are in the river.

I'm reading a book and
counting clouds.

I roll over
screaming, "Owee,"
reach into my pants,
grab hard at
a red ant
chewing on my butt.

The penalty
for crawling up my ass
and taking a bite
is death.

I roll him between
my thumb and index finger
until he is tomato paste
and flick him into
the current.

Pass the word.

Slickhorn Gulch

Clay. Clay. Clay.
The river is clay.
The cliffs are clay.
My coffee is clay.
We row out by eight,
leaving no trace,
no cans,
no litter,
no paper,
no ashes.
The footprints will be gone in three days.

We nearly lost the boat three times in the rapids,
stones that reached up out of the clay
to snag the chine, swamp the boat half full.
We bail with buckets, coffee cans, sponges,
and clatter down the rapids
fending off the cliffs.

We can't row through Government Rapid.
We carry 600 pounds of gear downriver
and rope the boat through the suck and gush.
It's strong, the river,
stronger that I thought.

We row 8 hours,
24 miles,
18 rapids
and a 100 side canyons.
The crows follow us along.

We are news.
We have a boat full of food.

The crows sit on the canyon wall
on the other side of the river,
squawk at us
and kick stones
down to the river.

At dusk
the cliffs turn gold,
burning magnesium bright
for ten minutes
then turn
back
to clay.

She Is A Room

There is a woman in L.A.
She is a room
with plain white walls.
Beautiful things hang on them.
She wears a dark brown rug
that accents the woods.
She has many windows
all with shutters.
They are closed at night.
And many doors, like any door
they go two ways
but they lock on the inside.
She has a name and an address.
She can be reached there
most anytime.
And when she's not there
there is a machine
that answers the phone.

When I dream of home,
when I go home
I go through the door
and all her walls surround me.
It is quiet.
She smells like eucalyptus.

She smells like sandalwood.
She is the only woman
I could ever be with
for more than a day
and not dream of planes
and sailing ships.

I leave often anyway —
thank god she is not perfect.
She can make me
throw keys through windows
and hit the wall with my fist.
I patch her with plaster
and white paint,
call her from faraway places
and say, "I love you."
She keeps the phone plugged in.
She leaves a light on at night
when she isn't home.
She keeps a picture of me
at age four by her bed.
I was a whole lot cuter then.

Lizard

Stone,
powdered blood
crumbling from the mountains
cascades
down the wash
to the river
cutting the canyon
out of the stone
in so many
millions of years.

I am hiding in the shadow
under the cliff,
the sun melting the sky
into little iron pellets.
A small lizard
crawls across my head.
Dry claws prick my scalp.
It tickles more
than feathers and fleas.
We are friends.

In two hours
we kill twenty flies.

He eats them all.

Steer Gulch

After today
the river is dead,
floating into
the corpse of Glen Canyon.

Its a lake now they say,
full of two-stroke oil,
beer cans and water skiers.

We still drift with some current.
The river is in no hurry
to get to that cemetery.

We don't row.
We don't talk.
It wouldn't be polite.
We're in no hurry
to get to our end.

Now and then
the river still
chuckles over a rock.

The last, sad
act of defiance.

Now and then
we dip an oar.

It's our way
of saying
goodbye.

The Way Old Rivers Die

For five days
the rapid stuck its fingers
in my ears.

A mile downstream
it's dead quiet.

The river is a sentence of Ss.
It is dripping from
a honeycomb rock.

It is old here,
dying.
It doesn't talk so much.
It's thinking about
a sea it will never reach.

It's tired here,
and slow
turning green and deep
and sluggish.

We drift
bit by bit,
turn by turn,
a cloud in the river,
a boat in the sky.

Now and then
we dip an oar,
careful not to splash.

A river dies without a whisper.

Clay Hills

It's the end of the road.
We drift into a sea
of garbage and litter
of candy wrappers
and beer cans.

The river is dead.
The current melted into the lake.
We have to row
to get somewhere now.

Thunder keeps grumbling
back up the canyon,
calling us back.

A river is a one way ride.
There is no going back.
The storm cloud
hung on the cliffs for a while.
"See you around," it says
and swims off across the sky.

The rain
makes footprints on the water,
turns
and walks
back up the canyon.

Gnomae

17.2.39 A Mind and its Reality are one.

17.2.40 The primary process of Nous is to impose order on chaos.

17.2.62 There is no end of horizons, no end of universes, no end of process, in the same way that there is no end to the detail of fractals in the Mandelbrot set.

17.2.63 Let us enjoy our illusions.

17.2.64 Let us play in our realities.

Bumper Stickers

Most men learn
ethics
from the quips
of basketball
stars,
and most men
learn life's wisdom
from television
advertisements
and although
no one lives
without a
philosophy
the philosophy
of most men
comes from
bumper stickers.

The Cabbage Patch

Most men kill
one another with
great enthusiasm
in the desperate struggle
to eat
one another's
patch of cabbage
and not even death
teaches them
that to win
the entire world
is to die
possessing
nothing
worth
having
not even
boiled cabbage
and to live
is to love a world
that no one
can own
or buy
or deposit
in some
afterlife
bank machine.

Teeter-Totter

Instead of wasting a single moment
on the passing of a thought
when the teeter-totter of events
see-saws from
destruction to recovery
and see-saws back again
most men
disassemble
the teeter-totter.

Another Day, Another Dollar

One Hiroshima happens every two days
all for the lack of turnips.
Fifteen to twenty million people
died this year not able to afford a Big Mac,
who could not find a dumpster full of garbage.
The Pope and Mother Teresa tell
all the babies to make more babies.
Forty thousand children died today
who couldn't find a turnip,
who never got manna from God,
who never paid taxes and never cast a single vote.
Now the world is safe from democracy.
Some of the bodies of the children who died today
will be eaten by other starving children
who will die in turn tomorrow.
Bill Gates made five million dollars today while taking a
         nap.
He will pay more than enough in taxes to buy every child
who died today a Big Mac and a Coca Cola.
Bill Gates will dine tonight on Ding Dongs and Cheetos.
After they were born Mother Teresa put a band-aid
on one in every hundred thousand of those who were
         about to die.
Mother T is in heaven now licking deep fried manna
from the fingers of the God of Love.
Some of the bodies of the children who died today
will be eaten by wild dogs and rats.
The dogs have high expectations.
The rats have got it good.
Homo sapiens my ass.

Dreaming Of Naps

My beard has gone gray.
I used to dream about sex.
Now I dream about naps.
When I see a beautiful woman
I just get tired.
A girl with a future
has no use for
a man with a past.

In A Sea Shell

18.2.1 If you think you have learned something, if you believe that you know something, if you suspect that you have understood what is written here, then you know nothing, understand nothing and have learned nonsense.

18.2.2 Make no dogmas. Trust no dogma. Do not believe this sentence.

Gulls

Dew, mist and morning.
On the grass field
a conference of gulls.

Wisdom and weather.

Stones

The great and mysterious
made men and stones
from earth and spirit
and from the winter mist.

Every stone,
like the face of every man,
is a picture of character
and understanding —

and like every flower,
portrays the wisdom of death.

For every man
a sacred stone

is waiting to be found.

Dusk

Dusk at sea.

The sun drops like an exploded orange.
The ocean is cobalt blue.
The sky fades into obsidian.

An occasional meteorite
plummets from the void.

In A Sea Shell

Poets believe
there is a lost word
that explains everything.

We put sea shells to our ears,
and listen.

The Piper's Night

The piper runs before our feet
twenty blurred stilts
churning sand.

We are in love, so we are
holding hands.

We believe we will live forever
so we are laughing.

The sun bleeds magenta clouds
across a bitter blue sky.

The sun bleeds to death.

Night.

Laws

You say
to punish the bad
and reward the good
stops the wrong doing.

I say
to make a law
is to make a criminal

and to reward the good
is to ask criminals
to make the law.

It is wiser to grow the flower
than it is to pull the weed.

Homilies

Homilies do not bring me closer to reality
and I have never desired eternity —
a fool would not know what to do with it.

Dusk, 2

The sun
a ball of French Vanilla ice-cream
melts down the sky's wall.

The setting is delicate, not spectacular.

The sea is molten lead.

Ideas On Angels

Emanuel Swedenborg had ideas on Angels.
He thought that to get into heaven
you had to be intelligent.
William Blake said that you also
had to be an artist or a poet.
These are both good ideas
but be that as it may, Swedenborg thought
that English Angels went around making parliaments
and that Jewish Angels ran pawn shops
and that German Angels carried huge, fat books
that they figured no one else could understand.

No one else would want to.

He also thought that the poor in spirit,
which, I take to mean lawyers and doctors and cops
and presidents and generals and bank managers,
never got to go to heaven.
He thought that they were just like hermits and monks —

they are simply unable to appreciate a good time.

The way that Swedenborg thought that Angels were made
was really one hell of a breakthrough.
Only two people who have loved
one another very much
could become a single Angel.

Their heaven is love and
every Angel is its own heaven.

Their shape is the shape
of two people making love.

I like that idea. It's nice.

It is the way we are,
you and I —

an Angel.

My Hair Dancing

The clouds cannot fill up the sky.

I stand at the window — watching,
a celibate light-house tender,
eye to the horizon
looking for the weather.

I prowl the streets,
watch my shadow on the pavement
reach for the sea,
the wind pulls at my hair
dancing like flames.

Sea air and crabs,
the salt crush of surf,
the distant invitation of horizons.
I stand at the shoreline — watching.

We live a moment
then die a long,
long time.

Empty Shells

A crowded beach is empty
as a deserted sandbox
if you can't find a shell.

Billions of sea beasts
live short, thoughtful lives
and leave empty shells
painted with the colors
of the sea.

I find a single shell,
put it in my pocket
and walk slowly home
rubbing its smooth, white
hollow with my thumb.

Ladies On The Sand

Ladies floating on the sand —
bronze lilies in a pond of sunlight,

their hips swell and plunge
to match the curve of shells

bellybuttons, carved sand dollars
swell into breasts —

soft abalone, waiting for love.

Ticks

The day is cold gray soup and fog.
The fog horn moans about being alone.
Being alone is the company of a watch.
The watch lays on the table
and the table magnifies its ticking.
The ticks slam doors on moments.
No moment ever came back.

Ladybug

Sweat and brush.

Sun's hammer,
heavy body
in the shimmering heat.
I doze
and watch a pile of ivy
breathing.

A ladybug lands,
inquisitive,
on my nose.

Marbles

The sun is sticking
its fingers
in my eyes.

I walk along with
marbles in my pocket
where money used to be.

If we do not
do our dreams
we die.

That is why
we do not dream
our death.

There is a universe
hidden in my pocket—
one marble in a bunch.

Even I

A string of events
leads to a certain poem.

The moment passes.

The poem is ink and paper.

Even I
must guess its meaning.

Open Wall

Winter gray dusk —
falling wet ash.

We dot the tidelines,
islands, with our backs
to the streets.

Cities are the jaws
of humanity.

It is easy to
go on breathing,
but it's hard
to stay alive.

We face the sea's
empty horizon.
For the moment,

alone.

Treaties

A stone knife cuts.
Fire lives in the wood.
If you leave us in peace
we do not need a treaty.

We do not need government
because we are not bad.

Foghorn

Night.
Black fog.
The horn
guiding the lost.

I wake up,
black ice morning,
get dressed.

In a steam-fogged
mirror
I write my name.

Headlights make shadows,
holes in the fog
leading to mirrors.

At sea the horn wails.
I burrow tunnels
in the fog.

In a mirror
my name slowly
disappears.

Gull Tracks

A gull's tracks in hard
wet sand.

Hammurabi's tablets
by the water;
hieroglyphics
I cannot read.

A telegram, unsigned.

Foggy Night

Fog horn,
full moon,
wind,
and the ocean,
whispering.

Things
are looking
at themselves
through my eyes.

Which came first,
this twisted
sea shell,
or me?

Lao Tzu

Lao Tzu on a bad day
rode through the gate
into the blue infinity
of the mountains.

A mind is not sucked
into nothingness
until every question
has an answer.

When a question
would bring wisdom —
a fool is silent.

Roots And Sons

Roots to earth,
sweat to soil.

It is better
to plant trees

than to raise sons.

Sea Horn

The horn cries
alone.

It is lost in the fog,

afraid we will never meet again.

It is hoping for a passing ship.
It will point through the fog
where land is supposed to be
and try to tell them,

there is danger over there.

Sea Marks

Curled shells.
Gull tracks.
Crab bubbles.

The gossip of oceans.

In the morning
the tide
has swallowed every trace.

The wind won't tell.

The waves are tongue-tied.

Sea Weed

We are that kind of animal
looking for meaning
in the pattern of leaves,
the twist of shells,
the configuration of stars.

The stars see this hunger
and run away
into the night.

The sea weed dreams
of deep sea beds.

Beach Drums

They are hungry for our trash,
smiling yellow in the sun.
A naughty dog exposes
the Coppertone Girl's rump.
Winter has gone
to summer camp.
No beer bottles,
hot dog wrappers,
no straws, no coke cups,
and no rancid french fries
hidden from the gulls —
the beach drums
are empty and clean
with a brand new coat
of bright, yellow paint,
stacked in the sun,
waiting for summer

and us.

Hurricane Season

Some, they say, have changed the course of human
     history.
Others never lived a day without pain and died young.
In the end, it really doesn't mean a thing.
There are guys rich enough to buy small
continents and herds of trophy women
and it's all as pointless as a Republican's promise.
If the world took everything you had and stole your
     name,
if you loved and lost
and every dream has turned to snot and ash —
it just don't mean a thing.

That's my life alright — a last gasp in a hurricane.
I might as well have never lived at all.

We are dying of thirst and all we get to drink is
a weak tea of hopeless obsessions and false heavens.

We are the only animal that knows it is going to die
and still, we pay the taxes and take out the trash.

I bitch and I complain. I piss and I moan.
It's as useless as an innocent dream of joy.

I call Brad in the nursing home.
The U.S. government and a Texas jail couldn't beat him,
but the Multiple Sclerosis is melting him away
like ice on hot, summer pavement.

"How you doin' Bud?" I say. "It's Michael."
On bad days he doesn't know who the hell I am, but today
I can hear Brad's grin, "Oh," he says, "Can't complain."
"Shit," I say, "go ahead. I do it just to stay in practice."
"Don't do no good," he informs me.
"You got that right, Bud. No one's listening."

One time, a long time ago, we packed up
our motorcycles and rode on down to Peru.

Now we wish each other love, luck, a day without pain
and we wait for some hurricane to blow us away.
Setting style aside, the simple truth is
we are both god damned glad
                              to be alive.

Trust

I do not trust a man
who cannot spare the time
to scratch a dog,
to pet a cat
or talk to a child.

His shadow is hungry
for the night.

He is late
for a meeting
with death.

An Old Drunk

The earth presses
the old drunk
into the sky,
doubling him over
unconscious
on a bus bench.
His hat
topples
into the gutter.

New Wine For Old Troubles

Summer came today
prying through the window,
spreading its bright cheerful cancer
like sweet jam on burnt toast.

Even before I can crawl out of bed
I want to be anywhere
but home.

I never liked asphalt.
I never will.

I get through the day
dreaming of pine and fir,
a few stones in a stream bed.

I remember the monsoons in Calcutta
endless dry dust on the Iranian plateau
dolphins playing in the surf near Thessalonika.

I am on the beach at home
watching the gulls hover in the wind
and speculate on the weather.

A few boats sail to a false freedom.

No matter where you go
there you are.

Lao Tzu On A Bad Day

I am 30 years as pointless
as a compass without a needle.

I shuttle days on an abacus,
forget my place and start again.

I always look
as if I am waiting
for some great event
to seize my life.

I will be buried with that look
stamped into my face.

I became
ignorant with learning,
poor with possessions,
lost when others named me.

Trust no god that offers salvation.

Lao Tzu on a bad day
rode into the blue infinity
of the mountains.

If things are done right
I miss nothing

and nothing misses me.

Plows And Guns

When man made the plow
he died.

Now others come,
plows and guns,
the open wounds of cities,
the cancer of fences.

It is our time to die.

It is time for the plow
to dream of digging
through our bones.

It never dreams
of the hammer, tongs and forge —

it cannot imagine
rust.

Poem Composed While Clearing
The Breakfast Table

Sick With A Virus, And Preparing To Teach
The Poetry Workshop

In this avalanche of words
a thunder of deadly silence.

We will not speak of
the transience of things.

We cut the azalea,
encrypt it in ceramic
and watch

until its petals fall.

The Mission Gnome

The sun finds her sprouting from cracked cement
and splashes her portrait on the mission wall,
a silhouette of Whistler's Mother in butter and black.
It is six hours to a free lunch.
She is older than caring.
No time to set the world on fire.
Enough time to sit in the morning sun
and hide her knuckles inside layers of socks.
By noon the street folk will be lined up,
gnomes fresh from the mines, around the block,
shuffling in the morning dust,
swapping stories about the cops.
The gutters blow dust and dead shoes.
The sun comes early, stays late.
The smog eats holes in everyone's socks.
This winter will be the last.
Right now, this morning sun and
buttered wall belong to her.
Six hours to a free lunch.
No hurry.
Nothing's Free.

Ship's Horn

Santanna winds,
hot and desert sweet.

At night I look
at the stars
and hear only vast,
irrational silence.

The stars are going
through the motions,
missing the point of it all.

Someplace in the dark
a ship's horn blows.

The Park On Skid Row

A hot day — sitting on a patch of grass
the smog chews holes in my glasses,
drifts through clouds of children.
The iron bench burns into my back.
The music drifts up from Mexico,
pours out of radio speakers
and soaks into the grass.
The old woman has been on
the streets for sixty years.
She never sits.
She hobbles around the park
stooping for beer bottles and paper sacks
chasing the afternoon wind.
Her friend sits in the shadow of a doorway
wrapping her feet in layers of plastic
while the machos smoke grass,
flex tired muscles, and shout
to mark their territories.
I sit in the sun just like the rest
waiting for death to take him, or you, or me.
It is a telegraph
this park, this wind, the sun.
I will die alone,
in a far away place
in shock and confusion
and no matter how beautiful
I see the world
in that last moment,
and no matter how beautiful
the thought that has finally

fallen from the edge of my mind
to the tip of my tongue
no one will hear
my final words.

Lao Tzu Selling Water

I write poems on the bottoms of stones
and throw them as far as I can
out to sea.

I grow careless with my commas.

Occasionally, to make a point
I will stoop to fact.

Job was wrong.
All is not vanity —
all is trivia.

On a bad day Lao Tzu
rode into the blue infinity
of the mountains.

But I persist
selling water by the river.

The Visiting Poet At The Dakota Cafe

I stare without a word
at the cluttered breakfast dishes,
not hearing the conversational
white noise that glues
the husks of our lives together.

When I said that eternity
could be replaced with the metaphor
of what was printed on the backside
of the very last calendar
the student asked if he could
use that image and I said,
"Don't use it. Steal it."

Poetry cannot keep me from empty plates.

The table is covered with
white butcher's paper.
Words cannot save me.

With a purple crayon I write,
"Between heaven and earth
the lone, black gull,"
and sign it —
                    Tu Fu.

Justice, Poetic

Knowing death
we invented
love —

and having
loved
we long
to
die.

Autumn Fugue

Autumn's tongue
of fog
licked
the fingers
of the dawn
sticky
with the sun.

The streets
are black
and gray
and point
to the sea.

The city
holds its breath
stays in bed
and listens to
the fog horn.

The ocean sheds
blankets of shadow.

A season
of dreams
comes to us.

Dandelion

Flo and I eat chocolate mousse
and sip our decaf coffees.
The day is clear blue and a little cool.
Love is the tickle of a light breeze.
We hold hands to the car.

On the tiny grass hill
there is a single dandelion,
a perfect planet of white fuzz
swaying on its stem
above the dark green grass —

waiting for the wind.

Most Men

18.2.17 With a magnificent leap beyond the boundary,
we make one another real by an act of empathy.
In spite of the lack of absolute knowledge we
choose to believe in love. Together we create
this magnificent world from chaos and isolation.
And so, the death of even the least of us,
diminishes each and every one us.

18.2.18 There are two things we are compelled to
explain: death and meaningless pain.

18.2.19 In our agony at finding no certain explanation
we answer simply that love alone redeems us.

18.2.20 By the grace of mutual consent we make one
another real. In that sense we bear witness to
and confirm one another's lives. And somehow,
in all this chaos of life and death, we love.

18.2.21 When a human dies the world is not merely
altered by the absence of one person among
billions. Rather, because the belief of a single
person sustains the entire world, the whole world
dies. In that sense, when a single human dies, we
all die.

18.2.22 There can never be incontrovertible proof
either for or against the survival of death.
However, both the human species and the
human individual are empowered by choosing to
believe that the mind is capable of survival
beyond death. This choice is based on the simple
belief that the Apeiron would not so conspire as
to allow the creation of something so
magnificent as the mind, only to consign it to
the trash bin of oblivion.

Do Not Dig Up My Bones

When I am dead
do not sell my bones
to art dealers
and literary brokers.

You did not want me alive.
You cannot have me dead.
I will burn every unpublished poem,
shred every rejected novel,
mulch unread philosophy
and bury every unwanted image
deep in a land fill to haunt
the dreams of the rich.

Don't piss on my grave
with your posthumous recognition.

Time enough to chat in hell.

You can't scare me.
Life has done everything
it can to pulverize my bones.
Life killed every dream
and took away my voice.
All life can do now is kill me.
Since that would be a kindness
life will make me linger
long past common decency.
Only the useful die young.
I look forward to my social security

and wait for that epidemic
or an economic Armageddon
or for the nuclear holocaust.

I will tell you what I have left.
I have a woman as sweet
as corn syrup and fruit cocktail.
I love her more than chocolate.
She loves me more than cafe au lait.
I have the sudden dance
of clouds in an ice-blue sky,
the sway of jacaranda limbs
in an autumn wind,
the whispering of the fir
on a mountain in the Sierras,
the geometry of a mountain
chipping away the sky,
the sweet melody of waves
licking up the shore.

I never gave up.
I never quit working.
I never stopped trying.
I exhausted every talent.
I never failed to give back
more than life ever gave me,
and still —

life wasted me.

And yet, fool that I am
I never fail to bargain in good faith.

A sweet woman,
whispering pines,
the melody of waves —

if only
sudden beauty
could save us.

A season of dew
and unopened buds
knocks at my front door.

The Last Straw

The dawn kills the dream.
The daughter kills the mother.
The son buys a woman and kills the father.
The boy breaks the woman in two.
The infant spits out mush
and kills the grandmother.
The girl smiles
and kills the man.
I was a boy once.
Today I remembered being six
at Bass lake, shooting
my great grandmother
with a silver squirt gun.
The sun is raping the night.
We are the false dawn
you and I
and we

are not dead yet.

Defensive Driving

25 Aug 97

From dawn to dusk the road is long.
My first day as a wage slave for TRW.

My key twists the ignition.
My tie is corporate correct.

Every crossroad reminds me
that I have lost my way.

Every red light tells me
that I am not in control.

I twist the wheel, depress the gas
and hit the brakes as required.

I have no idea who is steering the car
or what destiny selects my route.

It really doesn't matter.
I have bills to pay.

Bicycling The Strand
On A Crowded Sunday

Pumping the bike,
sweating the congested strand—
too much dodging and braking,
too many dog turds,
too many narrow escapes.

I can recognize the face of an idiot—

it is always in a crowd.

Bouganvillea And Rain,
The Artist And The Jaguar

History turned my art into posters.
Bougainvillea ate the roof.
Rain ate the posters.
Life turned my history into black fungus.
I never mattered anyway.
The ugliest kind of human,
old, fat and crippled,
angry at the world,
bitter with life
glares at me from the mirror.
"Bite me," I say. "In good faith,
I always tried my best."
"In truth," the angry man says,
"You never were good enough."
I think of Li Po floating into exile,
up the Yangtze on a barge
stocked with servants, rice wine and success.
I think of Tu Fu, old and dying,
alone in the night
sailing into obscurity and death.
I am sailing into night
immobilized on my recliner.
The only thing I want from life now
is a massive coronary before morning.
I am deeply serious about
wanting off this planet by dawn.
There is no excuse good enough
to face another sunrise.

Flo is out hunting for groceries.
My jaguar spirit hunts me in the night.
Flo buys me a small stone jaguar
and she brings it to me as a gift
and one more time
and for no good reason
she saves my life again.

The Philosophy Of Renunciation

Very soon I will stop talking.
Shortly after that I will quit writing poems.
I have nothing more to say to people.
No one wants to hear what I have to say.
They want feel-good poems,
they want happy, uplifting even —
I have nothing left but the truth.

Life the way I have experienced it
is not something people want to read about.
Besides, I don't want to tell them the truth.
I don't really care if it upsets them.
I just do not want to extinguish naivete.
Ignorance is the only chance for happiness.

There is a venerable philosophy of renunciation.
It goes like this: Life is pain. Stop being alive.

That's it. The best wisdom of the Buddha, Lao Tzu,
Shankara, along with three thousand years
of considered experience boils down to sentient suicide.

The only way to tolerate life is to kill it.

My own philosophy is simpler.
It goes like this: Life is pain.

Live it.

Only A Fool

I have learned more
from idiots
than from wise men
and more than
wise men ever dreamed
and even though
only a fool
does not learn
from another fool
most men
learn nothing
from either
and any wise man
can learn
from me.

LA Is Burning
27 Oct — 3 Nov 93

"Arsonists," the news android gushes over
LA's Dresden of smoke, charcoal and flame.
The cameraman loves the sunsets; lots of
oranges, brick reds, hot pinks, smoking yellows.
For twelve hours the news hounds chant the same
ten minute recitation and search out
gray-shocked men, women and children washing
the ashes of their homes away with tears.

They have come home to eat the ashes of their histories.
Some of them got burned saving their pets.
The history of their lives has gone from
snapshots and heirlooms to smoke and charcoal.

When they torch Calabasas I try to get to Dick.
He has a lifetime of negatives and prints to save.
The phone tells me all there is to know about busy
   circuits.
The roads are jammed with fire trucks,
blockades and horse trailers.

The richer the victim, the better the news coverage.
The richer they are the louder they wail.
The news androids circle their choppers
in a feeding frenzy of rating's lust.

If some madman had not burned down the rich folk's
   yard
some news vulture would have had to get creative

with his zippo and give new meaning to creating the news.
A dozen or so fires and 24,000 homeless.
No way we can watch *Home Improvement* tonight.

Too many brain-dead news androids.
Too many burning homes.
Too many real estate hustlers and building contractors.
Too many refugees from Mexico.
Too many obscenely rich men living in the chaparral.
Too many mouths to feed.
Too many babies in the oven.
Too many people. Too many people. Too many people.

Not enough water.
Not an ounce of common sense.
Plenty of madmen with matches and unleaded regular.
Some idiot tried to get even with the rich fuckers.
For days we see pictures of another rich fucker's
home overlooking the sea, burned down to sticks
and a fireplace. We get panoramics of the ranch,
burned down to a toilet and a swimming pool.
"Another million dollar home," wails the news droid
as if we should all weep big bitter tears
for the lost lifestyles of the rich and the famous.
The asshole that lit the match wasn't smart enough
to understand that the five hundred million dollars
that the rich fuckers lost will be billed to us.
Here comes another half cent disaster tax to pay
for Ali McGraw's home by the sea.
Here comes another rate hike for our car, house and
health insurance to pay for some trillionaire's ranch.
The price of a movie will go up another fifty cents
so we can all pay for some producer's canyon mansion.

The arsonist never even considered the little people
          whose
lives he burned to the ground and who won't get a cent.
Here comes another income tax hike to pay the fifty
          thousand
dollar bounty the state has put on the asshole's head.

He must have thought that bounty hunters work for free.

Nero burned Rome and blamed the Christians for it.
The moron gave us two thousand years of stupidity, foot
washing Baptists, crusades, inquisitions and conquests.

A Network CEO can never find his fiddle
when he really wants to dance.

Blind Fate And Vodka

The old man
shuffles
and canes
the streets
of Hermosa
like blind fate,
death with
a red and white feeler,
feels his way
along the curb,
drunk with vision,
he can't see a thing,
guzzling pints of vodka
through a dirty beard
slobbering down
his orange parka,
spattered with all
the blind years.

Waiting For Monica's Wedding
The Mission Ranch, Carmel

I am sipping cafe au lait deep in enemy territory.
The rich are sipping designer beer and dry martinis
and their babble is quiet, civilized.
I just got a speeding ticket
from a fat fascist on Highway 46.
There goes my license.
The predatory state is an incompetent parasite.
It kills off the host for trivial returns.
It will destroy a tax-payer's life
for two hundred dollars revenue.
I have never damaged
another person or another person's property.
I am a victim of victimless crime
and state extortion.
The moon is half empty
above Carmel Valley.
A light ray shimmers over the afternoon bay.
I can see waves crashing on Pt. Lobos.
The rich fuckers are intoxicated with themselves.
The rich fuckers never get a ticket.
They talk about killing raccoons
with their .357s,
brag that their cars cost
more than my entire life,
and analyze the relative
breast sizes of their secretaries.
In another thirty minutes
Monica will marry Kurt.
A joyous occasion,

auspicious beginnings.
Flo is carrying the flowers.
I am a true Renaissance man.
I have failed at many more things
than most men ever dreamed of doing.
The rich are sweating success
in the afternoon sun.
The only wedding gift I have for Monica
is cheap advice, everything I know about life —

stay the hell away from Highway 46,
avoid raccoon coats
and do not clutter the earth with babies.

The Luckiest Man

Bad luck is not a mangled leg.
Going broke is nothing.
Catastrophic health is tolerable.
Crushed dreams can be taken in stride.
A broken career is just another day.
Two wars and Islam could not destroy me.
A gray beard and economic slavery are to be expected.
The predation of my fellow humans is standard
        procedure.
The back stabbing of the artistic community comes
        without surprise.
I have failed at everything in life.
I am the luckiest man alive.
I have a woman named Flo.

Every Step

Search every square inch.
Follow every path.
Examine every moment.
When you come, finally
to the center
of your life
every step
you take
is
away.

The Angel

My dream
is the myth
of self

and Flo

is the Angel
of my dream.

One Way To Go

When you back's against the wall
there is only one way to go.

The Tiger Of Truth
for Jamie, born in the Year of the Tiger

Before you were two we went to Disneyland,
that icon of the atrophy of the American mind.
We all rode "Small World" twice
because it was your absolute favorite.

By that time I was a cripple again,
for the second time in my life,
and this time, for good.
I hobbled beside Tiffy and John
and he carried you piggy back
while we all sang "It's a small, small world"
and you smiled as sweet as angels
and buried you head in your father's
neck in an ecstasy of shyness and joy.

And so I knew that I loved you
when I understood that
you thought that we sang the song
just for you, because that's the way
the world ought to be —
just for you.

It is life's first and cruelest lesson,
that the world does not revolve around
any one of us.

But love does —
and we love one another in spite
of life and its hard, hard lessons.

I am old now, and tired.
More tired than anyone can imagine.
And you are a tiger, full of dreams and joy
and waiting to pounce on life.
You crouch in the jungles of youth,
tail twitching, eyes flaming
ready to leap
and I —

I am a sacrificial goat,
a small meal, and chewy.

When we had Christmas in Prunedale
and you were maybe five,
Rick gave you a train set
which was his way to say he loved you.
Everyone talks in a different language,
and everyone says the same thing one way
or the other, "No matter what," we say
"you can never doubt that I love you."

You and I spent a lot of time playing horsey,
and when it was time to pack up and ride south
you were sitting in the circle of your train
and goodbyes were being said all around
and I leaned down and said, "Are you going to miss me?"

and without even looking up you said, "No."

And I laughed and said, "There you have it."
And it's true. I wouldn't have it any other way.

So I am waiting for you,
here, in this jungle of dreams and lessons,
a small and chewy meal.
And you are just about to eat the world
and all that the world has to give us to eat
is stale facts, moldy bread and hard lessons.

So here it is:
First there is information.
Small minds love the facts.
Better minds find knowledge.
And the best minds seek wisdom.

But there is no Truth.

Truth is for here and for now,
for someone at sometime,
but never forever and never for all,
and never, never, and never absolute.

Only love counts.

Wisdom is a Twinky.
Soon as you eat it, you're hungry again.
But love is nature's most perfect food.

Hunt love.
Always give love away.
That way you always have more
love than you can stand.
Die for love every chance you get,
feed it to everyone you can.

I am sitting at my desk at work.
I am supposed to be doing something stupid
for no good reason,
so some moral cretin,
some ethical troglodyte,
some intellectual nematode,
some philosophical infant
can take away way too much profit.

Instead, I think about all the people
I love more than I can stand.

In the end, it is the pain
of those we love
that kills us.

I think about you,
hair the color of tiger stripes,
burning in the jungles of life,
prowling the forests of our dreams.

Some tiger has to make
the world a better place.
Too late for me, too old,
too tired and too damn bad.

Some tiger has got to get us to the stars.

You're it.

A Poem To Look Back On

I rise up from the ashes of my dream —
smoke and cinder and a flickering ember.
I can still stand on my own two feet.
I miss my life already.

These are my golden years.

I will never again believe the promise of a dream.
I will never again run, open sprint, knees high,
lungs pumping, just a single stride from flight.
I will never again walk into a room
without women taking notice.
I will never again stand at the base of a mountain,
knowing that no height is beyond me.

I will never walk upon the moon
and watch the earth rise, blue in a sea of stars.
I will never be acknowledged as a poet.
They will fail to print me in their anthologies.
They will omit me from their catalogs of greatness.
My books will turn to mold.
My pictures will rot in land fills.

Still, these are the sweetest years of my life.
The monsoons of my future have yet
to flood my days with their long, sad rains.

Almost everyone I love is still alive.

My brother, Rick, is almost healthy and not drunk in
        some gutter
or being mauled by some state institution or other.
Lance is still crazy, but living safe in Nana's house
instead of sleeping under an overpass and eating from a
        dumpster.
My parents are both alive and living on their own —
pilots of the recliner, masters of the remote.
When they die, I will inherit the earth.
A treasure I can never want again,
a prison with only one escape.
Tricia and John are secure in their northland stronghold
and my nieces are healthy and young
and rotten with joy and innocence
and an irrational belief in dreams.

Flo and I are tired, but healthy.
We work harder and harder for less and less.
Now and then, we decorate a wall
and walk along the strand.

All the young need to sustain them is the air they breath
and the jam of lies that life spreads on moldy, wooden
        bread.

In middle age we learn to eat our ashes and avoid fat.

The dreams we ate this morning
mulch the gardens of our afternoon.

Right now every moment is precious,
every hour is as sweet as the sun
poking its fingers through the pine

on a cool Sierra morning.

I sold my life to the whore of Art
and I cannot get it back.
I am powerless to make
the lives of those I love comfortable and safe.
I am impotent in the face of old age and death.
I cannot ease the smallest pain.

I am strung between two pines
beside the gurgle of a stream.
My life is an afternoon nap,
a lazy swaying in a hammock.

The stream, it seems, has plans of its own.
I watch the sun run away from the dawn.
I cannot stop its sinking.

After this —

      the dark.

The Last Word

18.2.23 In the final analysis, we choose the ultimate
belief; that there is a state beyond knowledge
and uncertainty. From time to time we have
given this state names and have attempted to
describe it. We have called it Brahman, The
Tao, The Great Mysterious, Apeiron, Nous, the
less offensive and more abstract descriptions of
god, and even the consciousness continuum.

18.2.24 But as soon as we give it a name or
description, it collapses into knowledge, is
bounded by paradox, and sinks into uncertainty.
And still we choose to believe that by leaping
that horizon again and again we may somehow
leap into the unknowable, into the ecstasy.

18.2.25 And from time to time we do.

18.2.26 And of that ecstasy, we can only remain silent.

Laughing

Everything laughs—
stones laugh
the wind, the sea
and garbage cans laugh
and pencils and paper,
molecules and galaxies.
Some things laugh
and don't know they're laughing.
Some people laugh
and don't know they're laughing.
When Dylan Thomas
drank himself to death
that was laughing.
Neruda laughed at the generals.
Christ laughed on the cross.
The nails laughed in his hands.
Socrates laughed
when they handed him the cup.
Lao Tzu laughed
when he rode through the gate.
When a child starves to death
once every three minutes
it is one more ripple of laughter
in the way of things.
We laugh at sad things
mad things
bad things.
We laugh at funny things
at thumbtacks on chairs
at Nixon on his estate.

We laugh when we are free
or when we are slaves.
They can't take it away from us.
They fear it more than guns
more than bombs
or tears
or being broke.
Laughter
is what you do
when there is nothing else
you can do.
It's what you do
when someone steals
your 63 Volkswagon
when you lose your woman
when you go to jail.
You've got to laugh
when you hammer your thumb
or stub your toe.
You've got to laugh
when you are sick
or broke
or tired.
You've got to laugh
when you are in love
when you win
when you lose
when times are hard
when times are good
when you are rich
and famous
and you own stars
and god asks you out to dinner

and beautiful women are dying
to make love with you
if you don't laugh at it all
you might as well be dead.
Laughter cures every disease.
Laughter is the key
to the universe.
It's laughing me.
It's laughing you.

So listen—
words are a blanket that's too short.
When you pull it over your shoulders
your feet freeze.
So if you want to make it
day to day
tell them anything
but keep the laughter.
Like when
they took Galileo
down into the basement
and showed him the thumbscrews
and the rack
and he repented
and said

"Oh yeah,
the sun goes round the earth" —

now that
was laughing.

A Lone Black Gull

Clouds above the Pacific
boiling up a storm.
A morning breeze
fingers my hair.
Seven minutes of silence.
Say everything you must.
In the end
the only thing
we can count on
is a hopeless
obsession or two

and a lone black gull

flapping
out to sea.

MICHAEL ANDREWS, co-founder/publisher/editor with Jack Grapes of Bombshelter Press and *ONTHEBUS*, lives with Flo in L.A. and is getting by. He has paid the usual dues of being a publisher, editor, and printer. He has been published in the usual number of the usual magazines. He has published ten books of poetry that were received in the usual manner, and produced three unusual portfolios of photographic prints and letterpress poetry. He has never sat at the feet of a Great Poet. Nor is he able to teach anyone else how to write poetry. He has never received a single grant, award or prize. No one else has ever published his work. He has sacrificed over fifty thousand dollars on the altars of art. He is not a professor of anything — and yet, he persists.

He has traveled around the world twice. He survived time in Vietnam, where he worked as a civilian from 1969 through 1971. He worked in Iran in 1974, rode a motorcycle to Peru in 1979, ran the San Juan River, and guzzled ayahuasca with the shamans in the Peruvian Amazon. His leg was permanently damaged in a motorcycle accident in 1987 and he now walks like a cheap imitation of Dustin Hoffman doing a cheap imitation of a deranged cripple. He has recently finished two books of poetry, his first book of philosophy, *The Gnomes Of Uncertainty*, five screenplays which the world will never see, two un-publishable novels, and is currently creating photographic and poetry montages as digital images while stumbling along on a massive novel about Vietnam and the boomer generation. To support these disgusting habits he works as a computer programmer/analyst, pays outrageous taxes, and suffers the usual atrocities of free market predation.